The United Nations
CONSPIRACY
to Destroy America

The United Nations CONSPIRACY to Destroy America

Michael Benson

CITADEL PRESS
Kensington Publishing Corp.
www.kensingtonbooks.com

CITADEL PRESS BOOKS are published by

Kensington Publishing Corp.
119 West 40th Street
New York, NY 10018

All Kensington titles, imprints, and distributed lines are available at special quantity discounts for bulk purchases for sales promotions, premiums, fund-raising, educational, or institutional use. Special book excerpts or customized printings can also be created to fit specific needs. For details write or phone the office of the Kensington special sales manager: Kensington Publishing Corp., 119 West 40th Street, New York, NY 10018, attn: Special Sales Department; phone 1-800-221-2647.

First printing: November 2010

10 9 8 7 6 5 4 3 2 1

Printed in the Unites States of America

Library of Congress Control Number: 2010925004

ISBN-13: 978-0-8065-3305-6
ISBN-10: 0-8065-3305-6

To the memory of H. Paul Jeffers

Contents

The United Nations
CONSPIRACY
to Destroy America

Introduction

The United Nations has got you fooled. No matter how smart you think you are, it's got you hoodwinked. The UN is an organization existing on the down low, using the opiate of world peace as deep cover—exploiting media control to create a dreamy good-guy legend.

It is, in actuality, an organization with a *shocking agenda*, more dangerous to the Free World than any terrorist group. This book tells you how and *why* the UN not only has failed to live up to its charter as a world peacekeeping organization and protector of human rights, but has become a breeding ground for conspiracies to undermine or destroy the United States. It also tells you how the UN has been infiltrated until dominated by representatives of enemy nations voting as a bloc in hopes that one day the Free World will crash and burn.

It should change its name to the United Un-American Nations, so dedicated is it to slamming us and our way of life. Some would say the bottom line had a cynical tone, the United States was all out of friends.

The United States may still have individual friends and admirers, but in a collective sense, we are friendless. Other nations are put off by U.S. domination. The United States is a rich and powerful nation, and the envious have turned bitter, causing America to be blamed for all the world's problems.

The UN was created to better humanity, and perhaps for a time it did. But those days, as this book proves point by point, are long gone. That

1

idealistic notion has been downsized into blatant anti-Americanism, often originating from countries that owe their very existence to the United States.

Take France, for example. Without the invasion at Normandy in 1944 and the subsequent liberation of France from Nazi rule, not just that country, but Europe and the world would be a much different—and worse—place.

But only two generations later, when the United States calls for cooperation from France in matters of foreign policy, the French collectively make a sour face as if they'd just smelled something bad.

The UN is now fully stocked with America's sworn enemies who have used that forum to unite with anti-American fervor. On the floor of the UN, there are frequent mentions of "Yankee imperialism."

It's an organization that has expelled the United States from its Human Rights Council while allowing Libya to maintain its membership. If it weren't a situation bound to have tragic manifestations, it would play as a comedy.

And the UN thrives, housed and sheltered securely on America's hallowed soil. And that's a sin. It was conceived as a neutral, global peacekeeping body. Now it overlooks the East River like America's tombstone.

The UN is corrupt. It's been proven, as this book shows, again and again. Even before the current swell of anti-Americanism from the Third World, the real motives behind the UN and its dream of New World Order was hardly pristine. There is more interest in profit than ethics.

Birth of the Monster

It is about time that the truth be known! The UN betrayed the nation that empowered and protected it, allowing anti-American thieves and tyrants to corrupt its mandate and its operations.

The international body that was formed with American leadership after World War II not only has failed to live up to its founding charter as a peacekeeping world organization and protector of human rights, but has become the breeding ground for conspiracies to undermine and destroy the U.S. economy in the interest of underdeveloped nations of the Third World, almost all of which are anti-American. You will discover that in the history of the UN corruption and intrigue are nothing new in those East Side halls.

From the very beginning the UN was a home for dreamers and schemers.

The UN was always supposed to be a spooky place, in the clandestine espionage sense—a shadowy world where many people, perhaps *everyone*, weren't what they seemed. The powers that constructed it were old and heavily influenced by some of the world's most powerful men and the near invisible world of secret societies. A checklist of UN behavior was frightening.

The UN's International Baccalaureate program teaches U.S. schoolchildren that they are citizens of the world and that love of country is evil. The UN is working to subject the U.S. Supreme Court to the International Court of Justice (ICJ). The UN Convention on the Law of the Sea would have limited the U.S. Navy's freedom to roam the oceans to protect the United States and its allies, a treaty that was denounced in Congress as "an affront to American national sovereignty." The UN is a body that has enabled bribery, embezzlement, and sex crimes under its banner. It has promoted socialism and globalization and provided a podium—a bloody soapbox—for such America haters as Cuba's Fidel Castro, USSR's Khrushchev, Middle East's gun-toting Yasser Arafat, Venezuela's Hugo Chavez, and Iran's Mahmoud Ahmadinejad.

Why?

America not only is harboring its own worst enemy, it is also financing it with taxpayer dollars. Our noses are rubbed in it as we bankroll our own downfall. Just as the peace love dove vacuole of the 1960s hippie movement birthed Charlie Manson and Helter Skelter, so the well-opiated UN birthed its own monster, its gift to the Free World, a demon of dogma slouching toward Bethlehem with the bloody wind of the Crusades at its back.

The Rose-Colored Glasses of Franklin Delano Roosevelt

A generation of Americans growing up during World War II often heard President Franklin Delano Roosevelt (FDR) on the radio. During those fireside chats he referred to the countries fighting the Germans and the Japanese not as "the Allies," as newspaper and radio reporters did, but as the "United Nations."

Not long before he died in January 2010, World War II historian and superpatriot H. Paul Jeffers wrote of his impressionable boyhood during the postwar years. He recalled that when the UN was formally organized, he had a small blue-and-white United Nations flag tacked to his bedroom wall.

In high school, Jeffers participated in a "model UN General Assembly" that was put on by the Philadelphia regional high schools at the University of Pennsylvania. When the Security Council convened in its temporary headquarters at Lake Success, New York, to deal with the outbreak of a war in Korea in June 1950, he watched the proceedings on the TV set, with a ten-inch screen, that his father had bought a few years earlier. He felt proud of the United States and the UN for rallying to the plight of the free people of South Korea who were being overrun by a horde of invaders from Communist North Korea.

Not long after the UN moved into its permanent location on New York City's First Avenue, *on land donated by John D. Rockefeller*, Jeffers joined other students for a guided tour of the headquarters and saw the Security Council chamber on the ground floor of the impressive and imposing forty-story office building and the General Assembly's auditorium beneath the dome of an adjoining structure with a majestic sloping roof.

In 1964, as a reporter for ABC Radio News, Jeffers occasionally covered UN meetings and observed public and private expressions of animosity toward the United States because of the conflict in Vietnam, which was labeled by many Third World countries as a colonial war.

The United States was also faulted, he recalled, by Arab nations for its support of Israel. No other issue before the UN, he noticed, contributed more to anti-American sentiment than the conflict between the Arab states and the Jewish state.

Dividing Palestine

Despite a UN decision in 1947 to divide the postwar British mandate in Palestine between Jews and Arabs, an increase in UN membership of Muslim nations resulted in a UN resolution that Zionism, which called for the creation of Israel, was racism.

It was this declaration that turned the UN from its role as a champion of peaceful relations between nations to a pro-Arab body. Because Israel could not survive without American support, the United States was seen not only as an obstacle to Arab desires to eliminate Israel, but as an imperialistic power that was the bulwark of capitalism and a roadblock to worldwide Socialism.

Cold War Fractures

This bulwark or roadblock view flourished as the UN membership list expanded in the decades since World War II, and the globe fractured during the Cold War into three blocs—nations allied with the United States (the West), the Soviet Union and its satellites, and the "uncommitted nations," many of them part of the Third World.

In the post–Cold War era, there was a realignment, and there was a brief euphoric period during which the United States thought its number one enemy was whipped. As it turned out, a new enemy, a slithering and insidious foe not bound by the laws of civilized man, emerged. It was an enemy willing to attack women and children and to hit and run. It was an enemy made strong and united by an extremist interpretation of Islam.

Through an ongoing process, the UN developed into a force that hoped to tip the scale from Right to Left, from West to Middle East, from First to Third World.

A 1986 investigation requested by Senate Foreign Relations Committee member Arlen Specter by the General Accounting Office (now called the Government Accountability Office) confirmed that the UN's public information operations were biased against the United States. A content analysis of materials produced by the UN's Department of Public Information (DPI) found that publications and radio and TV programs frequently opposed key U.S. interests, discussed U.S. policies in a biased manner, and distorted or ignored U.S. purposes at the UN.

Not What FDR Had in Mind

All of this would have come as a shock to the idealistic American president who reportedly envisioned the United States leading the UN into an epoch of world peace and prosperity. In letters dated February 28, 1945, President Franklin D. Roosevelt invited wartime allies to send delegates to "the United Nations Conference" in San Francisco on April 25, 1945.

He wrote, with his usual run-on abandon, "I feel certain that this important conference bringing together all the United Nations which have so loyally cooperated in the war against their common enemies will successfully complete the plans for an international organization through which the close and continuing collaboration of all peace-loving peoples may be directed toward the prevention of future international conflict and the removal of the political, economic, and social causes of war. I am confident that as a member of the delegation, you would effectively contribute to the realization of the hopes and aspirations of the American people for an international organization through which this nation may play its full part in the maintenance of international peace and security."

Because FDR felt the United States shouldn't belong to any organization it could not control, he made certain that the United States would have veto power in the Security Council, along with the other major powers during World War II—Great Britain, Russia, France, and China.

When representatives of the fifty nations convened in San Francisco to complete the Charter of the United Nations, the result was the establishment of a General Assembly of all member states and a Security Council of five permanent members (with veto power), and six nonpermanent members.

The Charter provided for an eighteen-member Economic and Social Council, an International Court of Justice (ICJ), a Trusteeship Council to oversee certain colonial territories, and a Secretariat under a secretary-general.

The U.S. Senate approved the Charter on July 28, 1945, by a vote of 89 to 2. The United Nations came into existence on October 24, 1945, after twenty-nine nations had ratified the Charter.

Notice, in FDR's world, enemy nations simply were not invited to the party. In 2010, almost seven decades later, the UN consisted of 192 members, almost all of whom had shown antagonism to American policies and resentment toward U.S. economic power.

Roosevelt did not anticipate that the UN's membership would expand through the admission of scores of small, poor nations, few of which were true democracies, nor did he anticipate that the General Assembly would become imbued with far more influence than intended and that the lavishly decorated public rooms, delegate lounges, private chambers for "consultations," ambassadorial offices, and nearby restaurants and cocktail bars would become incubators for anti-American conspiracies.

Good Public Relations

America was slow on the uptake when it came to the foul mess the UN had turned into. The UN's utopian vision appealed to schoolteachers, and the benevolence of the UN was taught in every public school in America. The UN was a symbol for humankind's high evolutionary state, proof that we as a people were more sophisticated than we'd ever been before. But it was a lie.

In some special UN schools, students were taught that the UN was God. And that was a big lie, one we'll get into in depth later on in the chapter titled "International Baccalaureate."

By 1999 journalists were beginning to get the word out. The UN liked to paint itself with a halo over its head. A closer examination always revealed budding horns.

Hotbed for Communists

Some journalists did not believe that the UN started out okay but turned evil. Some thought the UN had been engaging in a reign of terror since its birth. The UN's founders were communists, it was said. The seventeen American men behind the UN's creation were later found to be members of the Communist Party USA. The UN's first secretary-general, Alger Hiss, was later discovered to be a Soviet agent. The UN's secretary-generals over the years were all linked to socialism or communism. When it came to the big decisions, the communists usually won the vote. Even the American employees at the UN were socialists. Red-blooded Americans who were aware of the facts saw the UN as an enemy entity right from the start. Barry Goldwater, the Republican senator and 1964 presidential candidate, said that considering the makeup of the UN, perhaps it would be better if its headquarters were moved out of New York to Moscow or Peking where it belonged.

Enemy of National Sovereignty

The UN, with it utopian vision, didn't believe in countries and borders. It was okay if they took down some of the borders in Europe and elsewhere, established international currency like the Euro, but they seemed to think that American borders didn't matter either—and that was where they crossed the line.

The UN's World Trade Organization (WTO), for example, had usurped the right of nations to determine their own commerce policies by establishing its own foreign commerce policy with more than forty thousand pages of regulations.

For an organization that was supposed to replace bullets with butter, there sure were a lot of UN employees who bore arms and used them to exert military pressure on global sore spots. By the end of the millennium, it was noted that the UN was involved simultaneously in seventeen separate "peacekeeping" missions and employed soldiers representing seventy-seven countries. During the first half century of UN existence, it made war fifty-nine times, a statistic that flew in the face of the peace-loving reputation it was provided when taught in American public schools.

During the 1950s, the UN accepted rules of engagement that made victory in Korea impossible for the United States and South Korea. To tip the scales further, UN spies fed secret information to China and the Soviet Union, shattering General Douglas MacArthur's dream.

During the 1960s when the Soviet army invaded some of its satellite conquests, the UN stayed oddly mum, disinterested in angering the Bear (USSR) that was now firmly in control of Eastern Europe.

In the 1970s, the UN proved that it had no interest in defending human rights. Red China was allowed to replace Nationalist China as a member—Red China that used mass murder as a control mechanism.

During the 1990s, the UN flitted from scale to scale tipping the balance of power in favor of communists and socialists. In Nicaragua anti-communists were disarmed. In Bosnia communists were mixed with Muslims in the power structure.

There have been calls for the United States to quit that tower of secrets on New York's First Avenue and to boot the body off U.S. soil. But here we are, in the second decade of the twenty-first century, and the United States remains.

Helms Startles the World

Back in 2000, Senator Jesse Helms (R-NC) startled the world by telling the UN Security Council, "The American people see the UN aspiring to establish itself the central authority of a new international order of global laws and global governance. This is an international order the America people, I guarantee you, do not and will not countenance. The UN must respect national sovereignty in the United States and everywhere else. The UN serves nation-states, not the other way around. This principle is central to the legitimacy and the ultimate survival of the UN, and it is a principle that must be protected." Helms added, "I have received literally thousands of communications from Americans all across the country, expressing their deep frustration with this institution. They know instinctively that the UN lives and breathes on the hard-earned money of the American taxpayers, among others. . . . They've seen the majority of the UN members routinely voting against America in the General Assembly. . . . A UN that focuses on helping sovereign nations work together is worth keeping; a UN that insists on trying to impose a utopian vision on America and the world will collapse under its own weight. If the UN respects the sovereign rights of the American people and serves them as an effective tool of diplomacy, it will earn their respect and support. But a UN that seeks to impose its presumed authority on the American people without their consent begs for confrontation and, I want to be candid, eventual U.S. withdrawal."

Thoroughly Infiltrated

For much of the UN's existence, the most powerful and dangerous bloc was the Soviet bloc. After that broke up, the Arab countries stepped in to soak into the UN's very fabric. By 2009 the UN was thoroughly infiltrated by Muslims who might not be radicalized themselves but who would exclusively side with the radicalized Muslims over anything Jewish, Christian, or secular. Agents of the Muslim world lurked in every shadow of the UN building, undercover, some with Western backgrounds, white skin, and Christian names. One man with a Christian-sounding name who worked at the UN had, in a previous incarnation, been a speechwriter and advisor for two of the world's most dangerous Middle Eastern bad guys.

The proof of the Islamic bloc's power in the UN was how reluctant the representatives of the Western powers were to say anything that might upset the Muslim nations and their supporters.

Take the Arab slave trade, for example. According to David Littman of the Association for World Education, this problem was "one of the best-documented historical phenomena in the field of slavery and without which the various Arab empires could never have been maintained." Yet from the UN there was silence.

Sure Western delegates discuss the slave trade among themselves, in the privacy of a pub or on the street. But with members of the Islamic bloc around, they keep their lips buttoned. They wouldn't dare to say anything about President Omar al-Bashir of Sudan who was indicted by the non-UN International Criminal Court (ICC) at The Hague and charged with the "murder, torture, and rape of the people of Darfur." They wouldn't dare mention that, despite the indictment and the genocidal nature of his crimes, al-Bashir was welcomed at Arab League meetings in Qatar. Western elites, the same hidden government that had dreamed up the UN in the first place, were now scared to upset the aggressive and dangerous radicals who had infested the UN.

The Invisible Hand

Though the degeneration of the UN into its current despicable state is well documented, understanding the birth of the organization requires an alternative history—a hidden component not available in your high school textbooks—or doctoral thesis as well. History is all about connecting the dots, and you've got FDR, the man with the vision, and John D. Rockefeller, who "donates the land for UN headquarters." And you see that high-degree Freemasons had their fingers on the UN's buttons—at least at first. Clandestine meetings were all-important in the UN's history. There were also organizations that didn't make it into official history books, secret organizations, some fraternal, some paramilitary. Their underground machinations birthed the UN.

The most powerful secret society involved in the UN's creation was the Illuminati, the superiors who shed the light by which the rest of the world could see. They were presumed to be ancient in origin, and their legendary myths substantiate that. But their existence could be traced with journalistic assurance only to Bavaria in 1776 and the organizational activities of law professor Adam Weishaupt.

The leak of information from Weishaupt's organization gave the world its first glimpse of the Illuminati—men who claimed to command superhuman knowledge. Their intelligence was granted to them by a mysterious "higher source."

Weishaupt was an odd duck, thoroughly devoted to what he called the "ancient mysteries." He didn't use normal calendars and clocks. His Illuminati kept time using the Persian calendar.

"Man Is Not Bad..."

Weishaupt was a Bavarian canon law professor who'd previously studied to become a Jesuit priest. He became angry with the Catholic Church after Pope Clement XIV banned the Jesuits in 1773, and wrote, "Man is not bad, except as he is made so by arbitrary morality. He is bad because religion, the state, and bad examples pervert him. When at last reason becomes the religion of men, then will the problem be solved."

He described the Illuminati's pyramid chain of command: "I have two immediately below me into whom I breathe my whole spirit, and each of these two has again two others, and so on. In this way I can set a thousand men in motion and on fire in the simplest manner, and in this way one must impart orders and operate on politics."

Despite his hard-to-believe pyramid analogy, the structure of the Illuminati remained completely secret until Bavarian police raided its lodge and confiscated secret documents.

The Illuminati Order was outlawed in Bavaria in 1783. Because of this, many members left Germany. So the law against the society ended up unintentionally spreading the philosophy as new Illuminati lodges opened across Europe and in America. By the end of that decade, the Illuminati had ceased to function in Germany but had become a global organization.

Going Even Deeper Inside

The Illuminati helped disguise itself by blending with the higher degrees of Freemasonry. It is suspected that this process began at a Masonic Convention of Wilhelmsbad in Hesse, Germany, in 1782.

The convention was attended by Masons from all over Europe and presided over by the Duke of Brunswick. The blended secret societies became known as Illuminized Freemasonry and its headquarters was established in Frankfurt, Germany, a center of German finance. Among the founders of that lodge were representatives of the Rothschild family, the ultrarich banking clan often suspected of plotting to control the world.

Though the Illuminati became all but invisible once merging into Freemasonry, it is suspected that it continues to operate today. The members are said to be an arrogant lot, boasting, "We can turn the public mind any which way we will."

First Attempt at One-World Government—Denied!

The Illuminati planted the first seeds of a world government during the days following World War I, with the League of Nations, an organization made from the fabric of high society.

There were many elegant parties and dinners, and much expensive wine, liquor, and caviar were consumed. Even as the League partied the night away, a cancer that would come close to destroying the world, fascism and *Nazism* were growing.

And those tuxedo-clad delegates could do nothing to stop it. And so the League of Nations died. World War II happened anyway. The Illuminati with their superior brains had no answer for Hitler and his tanks.

Try, Try Again

After World War II, the Illuminati tried again, and this time the result was the UN. Just as the Illuminati had separated itself from its own history by invading the upper degrees of Freemasonry, it camouflaged its involvement in the UN's birth by nestling its plan nicely behind a cardboard cutout of FDR's utopian vision, and for a time the civilized world was all in.

Yes, for a time the Illuminati plot for world domination was near completion. It had control of all three branches of the U.S. government as well as the Western media.

No military in history came closer to controlling the world than the U.S. military in the splendid months between VJ Day and MacArthur's Korean invasion at Inchon. And the UN was there the whole way. Hey, U.S. and UN were only one letter apart.

Even Uncle Walter

The Illuminati's grip on Western media grew rapidly stronger with the electronic age. If you read it in the papers or saw it on TV it must be true—or so thought the people. Truth was, everything Americans heard and read was subject to Illuminati approval, even Walter Cronkite.

Cronkite was the CBS news announcer who for decades was considered the most trusted man in America. His involvement with secret societies was revealed when a reporter caught him attending a meeting of the supersecret Bohemian Grove, a meeting at a secluded campground in Sonoma County, California.

Once a year for two weeks, an all-male group of powerful publishers, politicians, and businessmen meet. Those who attend the meetings are sworn to secrecy about what goes on there. All information known about the group has come from reporters who infiltrated the meetings, sometimes posing as waiters.

Signs of Deception

The public believed everything they saw and read. The notion that it was being lied to simply hadn't come up. Not until the media sold the Big Lie about the murder of President John F. Kennedy that the screen of deception fell.

If someone had thought about it, the signs of deception would've been easy to pick out. But people didn't have the eye for deception in the 1950s. It was a naïve era.

Many Americans thought pro wrestling was a straightforward athletic competition when in reality it was sport entertainment with several layers of nonreality shellacked on.

History, they say, is the version as told by the winners, so the modern control of the media by the Illluminati is not a new thing. It is just a more sophisticated example of controlling the mind of the people.

That much power will always breed paranoia. The members of the Illuminati were not just powerful, the paranoid believed, but practically omniscient. They were also evil, satanic, disciples of the anti-Christ. Wavers of upside-down crucifixes.

Profiteers

Although the Illuminati had had a hand in the allied victory during World War II, the first modern war under its control was Korea—and that was largely through using the UN as a cutout between the Illuminati and the action.

The Illuminati didn't throw its power wholeheartedly into a U.S. victory. Instead it concentrated on keeping power balanced, staging small wars such as Korea and Vietnam, the results of which could be spun as earth shattering (remember the "domino theory") but which mattered little in the big picture.

These smaller wars would keep the military-industrial complexes on both sides of the Iron Curtain, busy, busy, busy—making a handful of men even richer and more powerful than they were before.

War spelled profits for the Illuminati. In this sense, much of the Cold War was a hoax, perpetuated by a common hand playing both the white and black pieces.

Maintaining Balance

The UN may never have been closer to complete control of world events than they were during the "police action" in Korea. At 4:00 A.M., on June 25, 1950, North Korean troops invaded South Korea, crossing the 38th Parallel (the political dividing line between North and South Korea established after World War II).

The Soviet Union supplied North Korea with modern military equipment: tanks, artillery, trucks, guns, ammunition, uniforms, and items needed to fight a modern war. The United States came to the aid of South Korea, both in the air and on the ground. That little wound would grow no larger, but neither would it ever completely heal. The United States' various aerial reconnaissance operations over North Korea started during the Korean War (1950–1953) and continued into 2010.

These operations continue to play an important role in knowing what that Communist country is doing. After a few years, the war ceased and was declared a draw. A demilitarized zone was placed between the countries under UN command. And when the profiteers had taken their fill, they moved on to another Asian skirmish, this one in Vietnam. And so on. And so on.

Korean Nukes

For years now North Korea was toiling to improve their nuclear program. It was assumed that its ultimate goal was to put a nuke on the nose of an intercontinental missile.

Occasionally the UN impeded North Korea's progress a bit by condemning this activity as nuclear proliferation. Of particular concern, the UN said, was that North Korea had in storage thousands of spent fuel rods (reactor fuel too radioactive to use). These contained sufficient plutonium to construct several nuclear weapons.

The UN, armed with U.S. surveillance photos, noted that North Korea's nuclear reactor was operational, and additional plutonium could have been produced for nuclear weapons construction.

For a while North Korea allowed UN inspectors in to look for weapons of mass destruction. They even allowed surveillance cameras to be set up at the nuclear reactor so the UN could monitor activities there. The arrangement didn't last long. North Korea booted the weapons inspectors out of the country and disconnected the video surveillance and monitoring equipment in the reactor.

North Korea continued to work toward joining the nuke club, and the UN could do nothing about it. The production, north of the demilitarized zone, of weapons-grade plutonium continued unhindered.

Is this an indication that the Illuminati is no longer controlling both the white and black pieces? Is the secret hand no longer ubiquitous? The answer would seem to be yes.

Endgame

Or was the UN and Illuminati cabal moving in mysterious ways, yet moving nonetheless, toward completion. It would seem that to believe in the Illuminati and a current role of dominance in world affairs one would have to conclude that the New World Order *did not* include a One-World Government, but rather at least two. The goal was not world peace, but governed conflict, a constant steady tension (and military consumption) that would require a very expensive preoccupation with defense.

As of 2010, Obama was on board. Under his administration the focus of American foreign policy may have shifted from Iraq to Afghanistan, but the Iluminati still had its little war that funneled money into pockets of the Illuminati war profiteers.

What was the endgame? As some saw it, the UN had new and unexpected difficulties with the Third World, but its goals remained the same as ever, to control the world, with one, white man, a king, head of the United Nations and with the Council on Foreign Relations (CFR), supported by a few billionaires, economists, and scientists. Followers of the new regime would be like pod people, and they would be called liberals. Those who did not get with the program would be enslaved.

As others saw it, the goal was to make a buck without the whole world blowing up. And as the Cuban Missile Crisis in 1962 demonstrated, the Illuminati organization was willing to allow the world to slide dangerously close to that line, the line between profit and doom.

UN Goals

Most of the UN's power hunger seemed to be global in nature. But did the UN (via the Illuminati overseers) really want to destroy the United States? Did the powers that be have a vision of America that didn't involve freedom and liberty and everything else Americans held dear.

According to the *Jeremiah Project*, the proof was in the pudding. They published a list of perceived UN goals based on real policies. That is they read between the lines of the UN Charter, then liberally interpreted its message.

These goals included the following:

- Control of all zoning matters in the United States and control of our national parks, rivers, and historical sites
- Control over whether women are allowed to have babies
- Control over the economic and judicial policies of all nations
- Power to raise taxes at will to pay for UN programs, no matter the size of the budget or the corruption in the system
- Power to force U.S. soldiers to pledge allegiance to the UN

No Comfort

But just as the Illuminati was undone by the Nazis, so it appears to have been blindsided by the new enemy, the terrorists of radical Islam.

So this is not a book about how the Illuminati control the world, although there is comfort in the thought—as long as we believe the group to be benevolent.

Even alternative histories are dependent on logic. And the logical interpretation here is that the Illuminati is losing its grip on the world, largely because of desperate Third World resistance.

Not all the revolt against Illuminati interests consisted of roadside bombs and underpants explosives. The enemy attacked the secret society close to home, at the UN. The attack came like a virus, wriggling through the capillaries of the UN.

The Illuminati's biggest fear in the twenty-first century is that the Islamic bloc will destroy the UN just as fascism killed the League of Nations. The only hope is that the current cancer is not as clever as were the fascists.

While Hitler's plans for global domination remained hidden for years behind the cool lies of his immediate disciples, the current menace commits acts of terrorism, openly targeting innocent women and children and screaming impossible demands at otherwise civilized UN meetings.

Knights of Malta

The Illuminati was not the only secret society that was said to have influenced the UN's sordid history. Another was the Knights of Malta, a group that developed out of the Sovereign Order of Saint John of Jerusalem (the Knights Hospitallers) after a Turkish raid forced the Hospitallers to move from Crete to Malta. When other groups such as the Cathars and the Knights Templar were being eradicated by the Roman Church, the Knights of Malta avoided this by aligning themselves with the Church.

As recently as the twentieth century, the Knights of Malta have been caught attempting coups. Two Knights of Malta were United States Directors of Central Intelligence, John McCone and William Casey.

In the 1980s, an Italian Masonic Lodge infiltrated by Knights of Malta and run by Licio Gelli became what was called by historian Jim Marrs a "worldwide fascist conspiracy." Gelli, Marrs wrote, was in cahoots with the Mafia, the Vatican Bank, and the CIA and was conspiring the overthrow of the Italian government.

In modern times the Knights of Malta have aligned themselves with the UN, perhaps because the Knights are a cover for actual members of the Illuminati. It is not hard to imagine the Illuminati infiltrating the Knights, just as they had the upper echelon of the Freemasons to better disappear from view.

Council on Foreign Relations

Another layer of camouflage between the Illuminati and the UN was the Council on Foreign Relations (CFR), "a nonprofit and nonpartisan membership organization dedicated to improving the understanding of

U.S. foreign policy and international affairs through the exchange of ideas." Or so they say. Who belonged to the CFR was not a secret, but what they do certainly was. The CFR published a list of its membership, but those on the council were required to take a pledge of silence regarding all CFR activities.

The CFR had a history that paralleled the Illuminati power play of the twentieth century. The CFR was born as an outgrowth of meetings conducted during the final months of, and just after, World War I. The nature of the postwar world was the subject of these meetings that were set up by President Woodrow Wilson's adviser Colonel Edward Mandell House. Out of these meetings came Wilson's "fourteen points." The points called for free and open trade between nations.

Institute of International Affairs

When the war ended, Wilson, House, and other influential men, including bankers Bernard Baruch and Paul Warburg, attended the peace conference in Paris. At the Majestic Hotel in Paris on May 30, 1919, there was formed the first attempt at a supranational organization, the Institute of International Affairs. Seen as a first step toward one global government, it was divided into two branches: one was headquartered in England and known as the Royal Institute of International Affairs, and one was in New York and called the CFR.

The CFR took the name of a preexisting but nonpowerful group that had been meeting at a New York dinner club since 1918. The first president was John W. Davis, who was J. P. Morgan's lawyer. This new CFR was incorporated on July 21, 1921. The bylaws of the organization stated that any member who discussed the activities of the CFR would immediately be kicked out.

Northeastern Power Elite

From the end of World War II until the present, the CFR has maintained its headquarters in New York City's Harold Pratt House, which was donated to the CFR by the Rockefeller family's Standard Oil (now known as Exxon). David Rockefeller joined the CFR before World War II and was elected vice president of the council in 1950.

Membership was by invitation only and consisted of what is often referred to as the "northeastern power elite." In the original rules, the CFR was supposed to limit its membership to 1,600 members, but in 2010 it was estimated that it had more than twice that many members.

During the 1970s the CFR stopped being an exclusively white male organization, allowing a smattering of women and African Americans to join. Members of the CFR have included several U.S. secretaries of state, including Elihu Root, John Foster Dulles, and Christian Herter. Another is Alan Greenspan, former chairman of the Federal Reserve. Journalists who are also members of the CFR include Robert MacNeil, Jim Lehrer, and Dan Rather. All three were in or near Dealey Plaza in Dallas, Texas, on November 22, 1963, at the time of Kennedy's assassination.

The CFR was so powerful that it often dictated U.S. foreign policy. And to believe one whistle-blower, the fix was in when it came to our democratic process.

After a round of public criticism from conservative writers, former chairman of the CFR, David Rockefeller, was instrumental in the formation of a new and similar organization known as the Trilateral Commission.

Council of Foreign Relations at the UN

Which brings us to the CFR-created UN. Author Ralph Epperson notes that the first U.S. delegation to the UN, when it was headquartered in San Francisco, included forty-seven members of the CFR.

Today's funding for the CFR is said to come from major corporations such as Xerox, Bristol-Meyers Squibb, General Motors, Ford Foundation, Andrew W. Mellon Foundation, and Rockefeller Brothers Fund.

As we've noted (see p. 17), the theory that best fits the facts is that modern wars are controlled by bankers and businesspeople rather than by generals and armies. Members of the CFR first took an interest in Vietnam back in 1951, a full decade before U.S. involvement there. That year the CFR created a study group to analyze the region.

The group concluded that British-American domination of the region was recommended. Three years later, one of the founders of the CFR, John Foster Dulles, convened a conference in Manila at which the Southeast Asia Treaty Organization (SEATO) was founded. SEATO committed the British Empire, the United States, France, and the Philippines to defend Indochina, a pact that led to the French and then the U.S. fighting long and bloody wars in the region.

According to author Jim Marrs, the CFR roster during the 1960s, which included Robert McNamara, McGeorge Bundy, General Maxwell Taylor, and Henry Cabot Lodge, was a "who's who of the Vietnam era." In 1969, Richard Nixon appointed as his National Security Adviser Henry Kissinger, a member of both the CFR and the Trilateral Commission.

White-Collar War

Continuing with our theory that modern wars are run by men wearing white collars, they would find it desirable to make the wars as long and expensive as possible—yet undecisive. With that in mind, recall that MacArthur (a Mason) was fired by President Harry Truman when MacArthur sought to win the Korean War quickly and definitively. MacArthur was a very important chess piece and thought himself above the demands of the secret hand.

MacArthur was replaced by General Matthew B. Ridgeway, later a member of the CFR. U.S. military forces in Vietnam were never allowed to use the full brunt of their force against the enemy but were instead handcuffed by "rules of engagement," which all but guaranteed a long and munition-consumptive war without a winner.

UN as Cover for War Profiteers

On the surface, the UN indeed maintained its utopian vision but there was no profit in a world without conflict. The trick was to keep the wars small and profitable without destroying the entire globe—and, indeed, during the nuclear age, the world seemed frighteningly fragile.

So, is it possible that the voices of anti-Western hatred are not the death of the UN, as the Nazis were for the League of Nations—but rather the irritants that make selling balm (and bombs) so profitable?

And isn't it that very profiteering nature, engrained in the UN's DNA by its father the Illuminati and its mother CFR, that allows the UN to grow so infested with corruption, negligence, and apathy?

Let's take a closer look at those voices of dissension, starting with the leftist voices of hatred emanating from the Caribbean and Central and South America.

UNESCO: Pumping Up the Noise from the South

The UN, on all fronts, is anti-American right down to its fiber, but we'll start with the "the noise from down south." Much of the anti-Americanism came from the small but pesky Latin American countries that have given way to a leftist government, with one lunatic after another in charge.

That noise was composed of the jacked rhetoric of overstimulated banana republic dictators and functioned not only as propaganda but as a diversion. The clownish leftist hyperbole drew the world's attention away from the real power of that Latin American leftist bloc.

And the bloc, this coven of self-proclaimed enemies of the United States, found cohesion in the halls of the UN. As we'll see, the Commie Cacophony reached painful decibels in one of the UN's oldest groups: the UN Educational, Scientific and Cultural Organization (UNESCO).

Attempt to Stifle the Press

Though the UNESCO's stated purpose was to help developing nations with their education, society, and culture, their actual practices flew in the face of that raison d'etre.

During the early years of President Ronald Reagan's administration, UNESCO tried to implement a plan that would require a license for all the world's journalists—a license subject to revoke by some lording anti-American commission.

The notion, which carried the official title "New World Information and Communication Order," called for a democratization of the world's media and more egalitarian access to information.

The reality of the idea, however, drained the blood from the heads of those who believed in freedom of the press. Cloaked behind the fancy words was an attempt to create a global press through which Communist and Third World countries could air out their anti-American ramblings.

Brainchild of Communists

UNESCO was one of the UN's oldest subsets, in fact it was almost as old as the UN itself. It was born on November 16, 1945, during the earliest days of the Cold War, the brainchild of communists like Alger Hiss.

UNESCO's stated goals had initially to do with repairing the educational systems of war-torn nations. At one of the first UN meetings—when everything was still warm and fuzzy, propped up with the daydream of "world peace"—there were calls for a cultural and educational organization to embody a genuine culture of peace.

Holy MK-ULTRA!

MK-ULTRA was a CIA program's code name for covert illegal human research, in other words: mind control, indoctrination, and brainwashing.

UNESCO was created to establish the "intellectual and moral solidarity of mankind." Its function was not only to fund educational programs around the world, buy books, and train teachers but to "build peace in the minds of men."

Some background: At the time of its creation, UNESCO had thirty-seven Member States. The ill-fated League of Nations also had a suborganization dedicated to the intellectualizing of the world. It was called the

International Committee on Intellectual Cooperation. Albert Einstein was a member.

Anti-American from the Start

The squawking from American leaders about UNESCO increased proportionately during the 1950s with America squawking about communism in general. It was a time of acute awareness and a time when the Red Menace was thought to be everywhere and artists were blackballed for being antifacsist. This too was a diversion, probably unintentional, that allowed the actual Red Menace to soak deeper into the American sponge.

In 1955 Lawrence Smith, a Wisconsin congressman, called UNESCO a "permanent international snake pit where Godless Communism is given a daily forum for hate, recrimination, psychological warfare against freedom, and unrelenting moral aggression against peace."

So by the time we got to the part of history where banana republics were looking to solidify their common interests, this was not a case of an old friend who later stabbed us in the back. UNESCO was anti-American from the get-go.

Scientific World Humanism

The first director general appointed to UNESCO was Julian Huxley, brother of Aldous Huxley. He said in his acceptance speech, "The general philosophy of UNESCO should be a scientific world humanism, global in extent...It can stress the transfer of full sovereignty from separate nations to a world political organization....Political unification in some sort of world government will be required to help the emergence of a single world culture."

In other words, the UN was seeking to organize the world much as the Soviet Union had, at that time, organized Eastern Europe.

Reagan Pulls Out

In 1984, as president, Ronald Reagan cited blatant anti-Americanism and hostility to freedom for pulling the United States out of UNESCO. Another unspoken reason was that UNESCO's budget was bloating at a fearsome rate, and Reagan, of course, was trying to cut spending.

A review to determine if the United States should rejoin UNESCO was conducted in 1990 by the State Department. The review concluded that the U.S. should remain out because the price tag for membership was too big considering the way UNESCO was known to mismanage their funds.

Abhorrent to the United States

Many causes the organization supported were abhorrent to the U.S. assistant secretary of state John R. Bolton—about whom you'll be reading much more later—who agreed that the United States should stay out of UNESCO. It was the right thing to do, he said, noting that "little or no" reform had taken place since we withdrew and that giving UNESCO money would be foolish simply because of the poor choices they made when spending it.

The United States remained out of UNESCO until 2002 when George W. Bush put us back in. During the time the United States was out of UNESCO, no American dollars went to funding activities, which should have been okay because of the nature of those activities. Instead the United States now footed a quarter of the bill for everything UNESCO did.

Anti-American Award Show

Among the activities subsidized with United States funds was the presentation in Havana by Castro of the Jose Marti International Prize, named after a Cuban war hero who'd been killed fighting for independence from Spain. It was awarded every second year in an attempt to "promote and reward an activity of outstanding merit in accordance with the ideas and spirit of Cuban independence leader, thinker, and poet José Marti."

The winner usually turned out to be an individual whose anti-American activities were considered beyond the call of duty. The first presentation marked the one hundredth anniversary of Marti's death.

Castro awarded a bizarre sample of leaders, cronies, and lunatics. One year the prize went to Pablo Gonzalez Casanova, a Mexican socialist who was the former rector of the National Autonomous University of Mexico.

In 2005, the winner was Venezuelan dictator Hugo Chavez, who was cited for his "contribution to Latin American and Caribbean unity and the preservation of the region's culture and traditions." One way he did this was by fighting American antidrug agents who sought to destroy his coca crop.

It was a big biannual to-do. Each time the award was presented, 200,000 people gathered in Havana's Revolution Plaza to hear Castro and the recipient speak. Mostly Castro. The ceremony, hospitality, and even the afterparty went on the UN's tab, with the United States paying a quarter on every buck.

So, if you remember nothing else about UNESCO, recall that they chose to finance an annual anti-American hullabaloo hosted by our archenemy, which was not just a great party but an opportunity for power-hungry anti-Americans to make friends, organize, and plot.

Why Did George W. Bush Reenter?

First Lady Laura Bush, during a visit to Paris, made the announcement that the United States was rejoining UNESCO. Mrs. Bush said that the United States promised to be a "full, active, and enthusiastic participant" in UNESCO.

The question remained, Why did Bush want to dive back into the pinko cesspool that was UNESCO? One educated guess is intelligence purposes. Why else use American tax dollars to finance an event that is intrinsically harmful to American interests?

If the move was to create an inside base for clandestine intelligence-gathering missions, that was one thing—and the result might have been worth the price of admission. The more common suspicion was that the United States rejoined UNESCO during the second Bush administration because it sought to answer back to critics of perceived American unilateralism.

If the United States wanted back inside UNESCO for intelligence purposes, did that mean an intelligence void was created by withdrawing from that organization for twenty years? Not necessarily.

Observer Staff

According to Nicholas Farnham writing for the *Comparative Education Review* in 1986, even after Reagan withdrew from UNESCO, the United States maintained an "observer staff" at UNESCO headquarters in Paris, which wasn't much smaller than the staff that preceded it. The U.S. observer staff was one of three on hand from nonmembers during that time. The other two belonged to the Palestine Liberation Organization and the Vatican.

UNESCO responded with weak comments to the legitimate criticisms coming out of the West. Concessions were always mealy and off point. Oh okay, perhaps UNESCO's budget could be trimmed of fat here and there. Perhaps the number of divisions could be decreased to shrink ineffective and redundant efforts. But say something nice about the Free World? Wasn't going to happen.

UNESCO did trim the fat. The organization reshuffled a tad. But as far as philosophy went, nothing changed. The UNESCO rejoined by Bush was very much in spirit like the one Reagan dumped.

UNESCO's Inability to Change Its Stripes

In 2009 UNESCO demonstrated that its self-image had not changed much, as it described itself as a "standard setter to forge universal agreements on emerging ethical issues as a clearinghouse for the dissemination and sharing of information and knowledge while helping Member States to build their human and institutional capacities in diverse fields."

The organization, it said, was to halve the number of people in extreme poverty by 2015, achieve universal primary education in all countries, and implement a global initiative to preserve and protect environmental resources.

As of 2010 UNESCO had 193 Member States and 7 associate members. Headquarters was still in Paris but there were a handful of regional field offices and many regional offices around the world. And it still financed the propaganda efforts of an increasingly cohesive Latin American bloc.

Axis of the South

By 2006 Americans were focused on the War on Terrorism, basically the battle to prevent terrorists representing radical Islam from attacking the United States or its interests.

But the nations of Islam were not alone in their anti-Americanism. There was also an "Axis of the South"—a group of small Latin American countries, some of them with drug-reliant economies. The UN, of course, has given that axis an open forum to speak its collective anti-American, hatemongering mind.

The Islamic bloc and the Latin American bloc believed that any enemy of their enemy was a friend. They'd learned to hang together during UN votes, so as to maximize their anti-American influence.

Just more proof that, as of the twenty-first century, the UN was intrinsically anti-American. How else do you explain the granting of a forum during the annual meeting of the General Assembly to Hugo Chavez, who for years has been doing everything he could to disrupt U.S. attempts to halt the northerly flow of cocaine from Venezuela.

Chavez had Oil *and* Drugs at his back—and he was a powerful man. They say all the world's power revolves around G.O.D., that is, gold, oil, and drugs. Chavez had two out of three, one of the reasons he was so secure, even when standing before the world and calling the leader of the Free World "the Devil." In the twenty-first century, the commodities that the world's power revolve around should be spelled G.O.D.A. A fourth item, the atom, needs to be added. The atom is only truly powerful when in the hands of someone willing to use it—use it as Truman had used it—to bring the wrath of God down on an enemy and not necessarily in retaliation for a blow in kind, but rather because it brings sudden victory.

The Drug Trade Half Trillion

Next to the illegal-arms industry, the drug trade is the largest illegal industry in the world. More than a half a trillion dollars are spent on drugs each year. The profits end up in the pockets of a few drug barons, and any representative of that country strolling UN halls answers to *them*. Most of the people depend on the drug trade for the food they eat and the shelter over their heads. The country of Peru, for example, earns a half billion dollars a year in drug profits.

Because of their enormous wealth, the barons are among the world's most powerful people, controlling the government of the country they live in. They bribe politicians and judges so that they can operate unhindered by law enforcement.

Dangerous Business

Manuel de Dios Unanue from New York City was a journalist who liked tough subjects, and wrote a series of articles about the methods of one baron's "Cali Cartel" in 1992. Soon thereafter he was shot dead inside a New York City restaurant.

Besides the threat of retaliatory murder, another difficulty U.S. agents had in attacking the drug barons came in the form of resistance from the highest levels, which brings us back to Hugo Chavez. In August 2005, he called the United States hypocritical when it came to the War on Drugs and said American agents were in the country not to stop drug trafficking but to spy.

The United States, he pointed out, was the world's largest consumer of drugs, and yet it did little to reduce the number of drug users inside America. While DEA and FBI agents were busy in Venezuela, he noted that they ignored the drug barons who were living inside the United States.

Clearly, the president did not have the right attitude to maximize the war on drugs within his country. Criticisms of Chavez's words were few from official U.S. sources. Remember, he had coke and oil at his back. Venezuela was a major supplier of oil to the United States.

Chavez's job when he came to New York in 2006 was to make George W. Bush look bad in the eyes of the world. But there was a flaw in the plan. Trouble was the world was a sophisticated place and Chavez was *not* a sophisticated man.

Chavez Calls Bush the D-Word

Famously, Chavez called Bush "the Devil" at the UN in September 2006. The name calling said more about Chavez than Bush. Chavez's insults to Bush were sometimes personal and below the belt. During another speech that week in New York, he called Bush "an alcoholic and a sick man."

Any political advantage Chavez and his anti-American allies might have sought backfired as even Bush's political enemies at home fought to be first to condemn the Venezuelan lunatic.

For example, Charles Rangel, a Democrat from New York, said, "Even though many American people are critical of our president, we resent the fact that he would come to the United States and criticize President Bush."

Raucous Carnivals, Shrill Displays

Chavez wasn't the only anti-American lunatic to speak before the 2006 General Assembly. Mahmoud Ahmadinejad of Iran also spoke, using the opportunity once again to call the Holocaust a hoax and to assail the "hegemonic powers for their exclusionist policies on international decision-making mechanisms, including the Security Council."

David Usbourne wrote in a British periodical that lunatic dictators "hijacked [2006's] UN General Assembly and turned it into a raucous carnival of anti-Americanism. It perhaps will not hurt Mr. Bush's domestic standing, but for American diplomacy abroad it was, at the very least, unsettling."

About the UN-sponsored hatemongering, Nile Gardiner of the Heritage Foundation added, "It has been one of the shrillest displays of anti-Americanism in recent years. This is a huge public diplomacy challenge, but also a strategic threat." Gardiner said the Chavez Devil quote was "the strongest attack from any foreign leader on U.S. soil in decades."

Ducks in a Row

In the days before the 2006 General Assembly convened, the axis of the South could be heard getting its anti-American ducks in a row. The so-called Non-Aligned Movement met in Havana, Cuba, where Cuba's vice president, Carlos Lage Dávila criticized "the worldwide dictatorship by the United States."

One thing crystallized during those days: America's enemies didn't always have a lot in common—Venezuela and Cuba were very different places from Iran and Yemen—but their common hatred proved to be a strong bond.

World leaders previously reluctant to speak up on anti-American, anti-Western issues were emboldened by the tone of the 2006 meetings. President Omar al-Bashir of Sudan, a man who might have previously held his tongue, freely spoke against UN efforts to deploy a blue-helmet peacekeeping force in Darfur.

Evo Morales of Bolivia joined the fray and Pervez Musharraf of Pakistan created an anti-American stir when he announced that "the United States threatened to bomb his country into the Stone Age" if he did not join the war against terror.

Coca Kooks and Shoe Bangers

There were incidents during the UN meetings that reminded historians of the infamous scene during the height of the Cold War when Soviet Union premier Nikita Khrushchev banged his shoe on a table as a form of anti-American protest.

Forty-five years later, a Bolivian leader used a coca leaf as a visual aid, waving it angrily as he spoke about U.S. attempts to destroy Bolivian coca crops.

Chavez was relentlessly ambitious and had a history of using the UN to boost his own power. He used the organization as a tool by which to move his wild South American chess pieces closer to endgame and the toppling of the Stars and Stripes. In 2006 Chavez also came with props, waving an anti-American book as he spoke, recommending that everyone read it.

Attempts to undermine Bush's support inside the United States might have fallen on deaf ears, but these dictators with their crude comments did successfully malign the Security Council as a "relic" of World War II, composed of nations that felt "entitled to world dictatorship."

Plans in Haiti

In 2010 Chavez still had a big mouth and was quick with the verbal barb at his enemies, but had he lost his hunger for power? Was he now content to be baron number one in Venezuela?

There was a clear indication that the answer was no. In the days following the deadly earthquake that tore apart Haiti, even as death estimates ran in the hundreds of thousands, Chavez was already spinning the story to his benefit, with an eye toward increased leftist power in Haiti.

The earthquake had caused a power vacuum—one the socialists, the UN, and the U.S. military were all eager to fill. Chavez used his own Venezuelan TV show, called *Hello, President* to launch his leftist scheme.

Chavez told his people that Venezuela was a country with a large heart and—with Haitians in trouble—wanted to help in any way it could. But that large-hearted effort was being stifled, stymied, and thwarted by the Americans who got there first. The Yankees, as he called them, had clogged up all of Haiti's ports so that Venezuelan ships, crammed to the brim with relief aid, were not being allowed to dock so they could not unload. It was an example of a typical American power grab, he exclaimed.

But the intrepid Venezuelan humanitarian effort did not give up easily. The ships simply moved to a Dominican Republic port where they were allowed to dock. From there the food and medicine were transported over the land to the Haitian disaster area.

He said that he had great plans for the rebuilding of Haiti. He personally planned to take a leadership role in making Haiti a thriving place. He would team up with Cuba and all the other like-minded governments in the region to build hospitals and schools in Haiti and set up agricultural programs. He was a progressive thinker. He wanted the world to know that and sought to perpetuate the humanitarian effort by installing a system through which Haitians could feed themselves forever.

The left-leaning leaders of Latin America were working with a regional trade group called the Bolivarian Alliance for the Americas (ALBA) to fix Haiti. ALBA was looking for contributions, Chavez noted.

Before finishing his little chat with the nation, Chavez got in one last slam at the Yankees, claiming that the Pentagon was using the earthquake as an excuse to occupy Haiti. He called the disaster area a "battlefield." Chavez promised he would not allow "the gringo empire to take over Haiti."

Most of this was a crock, although it was confirmed that Venezuela did contribute some food and oil to Haiti. Chavez hungered for power, there could be no question about that, but the sort of power he sought needed a bite that an appearance on the *Hello, President* TV show couldn't muster. He knew that, even with the UN on his side, he'd been rendered weak in Haiti, and he wanted to make sure his people knew that he was still a strong man and that they should never forget who the good guys and the bad guys were.

Spies, Hypocrites, and Deadbeats

Another reason to quit the UN and boot its headquarters the hell out of New York City was the financial drain on the Big Apple of hosting the world's corrupt and ill-mannered diplomats. Not only were they scofflaws, but many of them were espionage agents, running their ops on our dime—sometimes with a police escort!

Protected by diplomatic immunity, the foreign embassies in New York have served since the UN's birth as home bases for espionage, housing diplomat/agents who simultaneously stole our secrets, consistently promoted anti-Americanism in the UN, and arrogantly abused their roles as emissaries.

They ran up the tab by tying up traffic with motorcades, ignoring the city's parking laws, and refusing to pay millions of dollars in fines. They used their special postal privileges to mail secret microfilm back to their home government.

Global Spy vs. Spy

Nobody is surprised when they learn the UN is—was, and always will be—a hotbed for imbedded secret agents, professional learners of secrets. Everyone knows that during the Cold War the CIA and KGB matched wits in a global game of Spy vs. Spy. This massive behind-the-scenes confrontation, though it did sometimes resemble the cartoons in *Mad*

Magazine, seeped into all the nooks and crannies of world politics, until it was part of the infrastructure. One side tried to yank secrets from the opponent. The other side blocked that yank and went on information quests of its own.

Then the Berlin Wall came down. The Soviet Union lost its hold and became Russia and its neighbors. The Cold War was over. So what happened to all those clandestine agents infiltrating the other side and the double agents who gathered information for either side?

Did those global intelligence-gathering machines dissolve and soak into the earth? Did they disassemble in an orderly manner as the KGB supposedly did? Were they instantly transferred and seamlessly adjusted to a new enemy as the CIA supposedly did? Hardly.

Not only did the existing mechanisms of espionage largely remain in place when the Cold War ended, but many of those undercover operatives stayed on the job, converting into freelance spies, perhaps working for a client in search of financial rewards—a client birthed from the loins of financial, industrial, trade, and cyber trickeration.

Selling Out

Agent after agent saw the end coming and jumped ship like a rat on the *Titanic*. These supposedly patriotic operatives sold out quickly. Hard to believe for some, but the false assumption was that these agents had strong patriotic feelings in the first place.

In truth they were men and women on an adventure in which the question "Why?" was seldom asked. They rather easily broke down and became information whores, forming the still largely secret world of international industrial espionage.

They remained extremely well educated, these spies, and the Holy Grail became economic intelligence and proprietary business information, perhaps new technology that would revolutionize whatever markets their clients were in.

In the old days the secrets were secrets forever, and the fruits of the clandestine battles often died along with the operatives who fought for them. Some believe today's McGuffins eventually become known to everyone, a new smaller personal music-playing system or a phone that also can be used as a spy camera. Many of us own them.

Or is the game more complicated than that? In the world of intelligence, complicated goes without saying.

UN Hotbed for the Covert Orgy

The world of intelligence brings us to the UN, always a home for a wide array of clandestine activities. There was a time when UN publicity tried to avoid the notion that they were infiltrated to the gills with secret agents, when "intelligence" was a dirty word, but with time the UN adjusted to the assumption that spies were there, and less was done because everyone was suspicious of everyone else across the board.

Oh yes, there was a time when if you suggested to a UN official that the UN building was tapped and wired and filled with spies, you would have gotten a blustery guffaw in return. The very idea was outrageous. You were mistaking real life for a James Bond movie. It would have been much the same if you had told a pro wrestler of that same era that his sport was fake. Over the years, however, the blustering died down. As scholar Simon Chesterman put it in the *Michigan Journal of International Law*, "Outraged rhetoric has long been contradicted by widespread practice."

During the Cold War, people hesitated even to mention that intelligence gathering existed. The cover story was the only one used. So it must have been stunning to old-timers to learn that George W. Bush was publicly using the term "gathered intelligence," which he called by that name, as an intricate part to the buildup to the second war in Iraq.

Five Hundred Spies in One UN Building

To tell the truth, it is an understatement that spies were there from the birth of the UN. They were there before, already present and observing even when the UN Charter was founded. It is said that when the UN took its first votes, the major powers already knew the positions of every member.

Jerry Brewer, the vice president of Criminal Justice International Associates, said that from 1948 until the present, there had been five hundred or so KGB or GRU (also Russian) agents working in UN headquarters in New York. That is not the number of agents employed by the UN around the world. That number would be immense. This is just the number of Soviet and Russian spies who have worked in that one building—one building on U.S. soil.

"Crawling with Spies"

According to Ian Davis and David Isenberg writing for the *Global Policy Forum*, during the Cold War, UN headquarters was "crawling with spies," with just as many from the Soviet Union as from the United States: male, female, young, and old. Some were seemingly American and some were seemingly Russian, who were specialists and sex lures.

During Security Council meetings, both sides would employ lipreading linguists who could determine and pass along what was being said in private by the other side during tough negotiations.

Thoroughly infiltrated by spies from both sides were the UN committee rooms, the press gallery, the Secretariat, and even the library, which was a common drop-off point for intercepted messages and politically sensitive documents.

According to Brewer, post–Cold War spies who formerly visited each other on opposite sides of the Berlin Wall were now working in the UN building, and the intelligence they were gathering only pretended to be "economic, scientific, technological, and financial," when in reality it remained political. Agents came with "biographical and geographical specialization to make appropriate threat assessments and implement ways of neutralizing, dismantling, and eliminating those threats."

Brewer said that it was wrong for the U.S. and the other Western powers to focus their attention exclusively on the War on Terror and the threat of radical Islam because this gave too much leeway to the Latin American bloc, allowing it to rapidly gel and get its act together.

Was there any chance of limiting the amount of clandestine activity inside UN headquarters? Slim to none. According to Chesterman, "While there is little prospect for limiting collection of intelligence beyond activities that can be physically intercepted or prevented, increasing recourse to intelligence in multilateral forums is beginning to impose procedural constraints on the purposes for which the intelligence may be employed."

Sergei Tretyakov: UN Spy

In 2008 a spy named Sergei Tretyakov and former *Washington Post* reporter Pete Earley published a book called *Comrade J: The Untold Secrets of Russia's Master Spy in America After the End of the Cold War*. During the Cold War, Tretyakov wrote that he was a KGB agent.

When the Soviet Union dissolved, the KGB supposedly dissolved with it—but in reality it merely changed its name and continued operating. Tretyakov didn't even miss a paycheck. His cover was as a press officer working with the Russian mission to the UN in New York.

Tretyakov, in fact, led a small team of operatives whose job was to learn as much as they could from inside the U.S. contingent. Other countries were targeted as well, but the United States was always the primary target.

In most cases when sophisticated Russian operatives went to work on their American marks, the results were not good for Uncle Sam, but this story had a happy ending. In 2000 Tretyakov became one of the highest-ranking Russian intelligence officers ever to defect to the United States.

That record (for highest-ranking defector) still belonged to Arkady

Shevchenko, an under secretary-general of the UN who defected. In the 1970s he was a double agent who spied for the Soviets undercover at the UN even while employed by U.S. intelligence.

Spies Never Relax

Pete Earley, interviewed on National Public Radio, said that he hoped the book he'd cowritten with the Russian spy would function as a "wake-up call for America." He said Americans were naïve and believed that they could relax when the Cold War ended. "That wasn't the case with intelligence work," he said. Spies never relaxed.

When Tretyakov defected to the United States, he brought with him a treasure trove of information from within the big Russian intelligence machine. More than five thousand top secret Russian documents were turned over to the United States exposing and ruining myriad complex Russian operations.

Tretyakov said, "My defection was *the* major failure of the Russian intelligence, probably in all of history."

He denied having a mercenary bone in his body and admitted forfeiting an inheritance equivalent to millions of dollars when he defected. He said it was never about the money. It was about his disillusionment with the Russian system.

"I never asked for a penny from any foreign government," the former UN spy claims. He did what he did then, and he was doing what he was doing now because he felt obligated to "do something good" with his life.

The Men from U.N.C.L.E.

Of course, it went both ways. When the UN building in New York was thoroughly wired and tapped for omniscient electronic surveillance, it was the guys in the U.S. intelligence agencies who were posing as the electricians or the guys who were "putting the phones in."

This fact was known by many and assumed by many others in 2003. And yet there were exclamations of shock from UN officials who should have known better when, in 2003, a National Security Agency (NSA) plan to eavesdrop on members of the UN Security Council surfaced. The targets for the "Big Ears" plan were members that the UN feared were plotting against U.S. interests during the run-up to the second war in Iraq. The report was headline news in Europe (especially Moscow) and Australia but caused barely a ripple in Washington, where the "By Any Means Necessary" flag was up.

Agents of Islam

The United State, it would seem, had not completely coerced its former enemy in Moscow into a trusting relationship. But because of the immediate threat from radical Islam, the United States could no longer focus on Russia, not to mention China and Latin America.

It would be unfair to compare the intelligence-gathering capabilities of Third World nations to that of Russia, which inherited quite a sophisticated piece of spy machinery from the defunct USSR. But that didn't mean there weren't any Arab spies.

In June 2002 the United States ordered the expulsion from the UN of Abdul Rahman Saad, an Iraqi diplomat/spy who'd been caught by U.S. authorities while recruiting Americans to work for him.

Mistrust and Distrust

Just about every member of the UN had some sort of intelligence-gathering capability, and all of them utilized that capability within the walls of the UN. Taking this into consideration, you can understand that the UN often appeared to take the long route to a solution; negotiations seemed to go from point A to point B via Triple Z. It was because no one could trust anyone, ever.

Many UN representatives spent far too much time spending their trust where it wasn't deserved, while being suspicious of true brethren. That diplomat standing next to you may be your sister, whose ideologies match yours. Or she may be a spook, whose presence there at your side is deceptive, a honey trap designed to get you to part with your deepest secrets. And that was true no matter what UN country you represented. It was amazing, with all of that deception and espionage going on, that anything ever was done at all.

Oh, that's right. It isn't.

Scofflaws

Although it may tend to be overlooked by those taking in the big picture, the UN is a drain on New York City in small ways as well because of scofflaws. UN employees often have "diplomatic immunity," meaning they are not subject to American law. And many of those legally immune diplomats enjoyed being anarchists who were exploiting the lawlessness of their world.

As mentioned early, they parked their UN vehicles wherever they wanted to (running up an annual bill of $18 million in unpaid fines), partook openly in illegal vice, and committed violent crimes against women. There was nothing the New York City Police Department could do about it. From the boardrooms of major corporations to Manhattan's drug dens and whorehouses, the UN left its malignant polyps.

Even when not breaking any laws, their sense of privilege was corrosive to the quality of life in the Big Apple. Scheduling motorcades for rush hour and tying up motorists and New York traffic police so a foreign dignitary could get to his destination without being slowed by red lights were common abuses.

In January 2010 New York representative Anthony D. Weiner called out the diplomats of the UN to pay their bills. "It's insulting to all New Yorkers that countries like Yemen, Zimbabwe, and Iran owe the city millions in unpaid parking tickets. Diplomats park illegally, ignore paying their parking tickets, and expect New Yorkers to pick up the tab. This needs to end," Weiner said.

A study showed that Egypt was the worst offender, racking up 17,633 parking tickets between 1997 and 2009. That amounted to almost two million dollars. Weiner suggested that the U.S. simply take the two million dollars from its foreign-aid package and write New York City a check. For the record, after Egypt, the worst parking scofflaws were Kuwait, Nigeria, Indonesia, Brazil, Morocco, Pakistan, Senegal, Sudan, and Angola. As Weiner said, their bills should be paid in the same fashion.

Deadbeat USA?

Perhaps the best way to beat the deadbeats was to become deadbeats ourselves. What would happen if the goose stopped laying those golden eggs? We get an inkling of the answer in a 2009 statement by UN secretary-general Ban Ki-moon who, during a discussion with members of the U.S. Congress, noted that the United States had fallen behind in paying its UN dues. They owed $1 billion and soon that figure would go up to $1.6 billion.

The secretary-general actually used the word—he called the United States "deadbeats." The statement caused White House press secretary Robert Gibbs to say during one daily briefing, "I would note for the secretary-general that his word choice was unfortunate, given the fact that the American taxpayer is the largest contributor to the UN."

Ban never did withdraw his comment. He called it a "misunderstanding." At a subsequent press conference, the secretary-general said that he had "while speaking with a group of members of the House of Representatives" in fact mentioned the amount of money the United States was behind in its dues, "at the same time I noted that the United States generously supports the work of the UN, both in assessed and voluntary contributions. I noted that the United States is our largest donor. I enjoy an excellent working relationship with the United States and appreciate the many ways it supports the UN. I also noted that the United States is our largest debtor with a very large sum of amount in arrears and that it is very difficult to conduct smoothly all these peacekeeping operations and other activities of the UN."

Nothing in Return

What the secretary-general should have been talking about instead was that not only was the United States the UN's largest contributor, but it held that role for sixty-four consecutive years, *every year* of the UN's existence. The numbers were astounding. The United States paid for a quarter of the UN's peacekeeping budget. The United States paid 22 percent of the entire UN budget.

Yet all that generosity bought the United States nothing. The United States received the same number of votes in many UN decisions as the countries that contributed less than $22,000 per year to the UN.

Secretary-General Ban was not in the habit of insulting the United States. Some of his predecessors in that position had been, but not Ban. His deadbeat comment wasn't part of a larger program to irritate the United States. During the press conference in which he called his use of the D-word a misunderstanding, he also voiced his support for Obama's decision to send additional troops into Afghanistan. It was theorized that Ban used the controversial word to draw attention away from the fact that the UN's budget was out of control, increasing by close to 200 percent over a five-year period. And what kind of bang does the world get for that buck? Barely a poof. The UN had long been known for pouring money into seemingly just causes without much being accomplished.

We're deadbeats? As reporter Joseph Klein put it, "Let the UN's swarm of parasites make up the difference."

International Baccalaureate Program

One of the UN's most insidious methods of hurting America is breaking down patriotism, using schools inside the United States as a forum for anti-American brainwashing.

The UN's International Baccalaureate (IB) program teaches U.S. schoolchildren that they are citizens of the world and that love of country is an evil that must be abolished.

The IB is an international education system designed under the auspices of UNESCO and founded in 1968 by a non-government organization (NGO). These are the technically private ventures that the UN pays for. They sometimes exist only to do the UN's dirty work and perpetuate its nefarious program. In this case, the NGO was called the IB Organization (IBO), headquartered in Geneva, Switzerland.

The 1968 plan merely called for a school that would crank out future UN diplomats, but the idea quickly expanded until it became a global purveyor of one-world government Kool-Aid. Today there are an estimated 1,700 IBO schools worldwide, more than a third in the U.S.

Huxley Said It Best

The first batch of that Kool-Aid was mixed up by Julian Huxley. Huxley once said, "A central conflict of our times is that between nationalism and internationalism, between the concept of many national sovereignties and one-world sovereignty."

"The moral of UNESCO is clear. The task laid upon it of promoting peace and security can never be wholly realized through the means assigned to it—education, science, and culture. It must envisage some form of world political unity.... Specifically, in its educational program it can stress the ultimate need for world political unity and familiarize all peoples with the implications of the transfer of full sovereignty from separate nations to a world organization."

This is the same UNESCO that, as we've seen, was so un-American that Reagan quit the organization during the 1980s, the same organization that created an award and allowed Fidel Castro to decide who would receive it.

Global Education

It was part of the UN's utopian dream that all children everywhere in the world receive the same education. The trouble with the idea is that, when implemented, it pigeonholed students in the United States and ninety other countries to a common mindset.

And that mindset believed the United States and Israel to be responsible for the world's ills. The IB curriculum is close to identical wherever it is taught. The IBO is proud of the fact that all its students around the world take identical exams on the same day.

Yes, the textbooks being used in the United States are precisely the same—although, of course, in a different language—as those being used at the Tehran International School in Iran.

All of the exams are graded in Geneva. Grading is based on an international standard. All IBO teachers have been specially trained by the IBO, often at the expense of taxpayers in the local school district.

That curriculum couldn't be more un-American. Students in the United States are encouraged to "think globally," being taught that they are citizens of the world. Allegiance to the world supersedes national patriotism, children are taught.

American students who attend IBO schools don't recite the Pledge of Allegiance, and they are taught that the Pledge of Allegiance is wrong. What it teaches is allegiance to the UN.

The core themes of an IBO education include Theory of Knowledge, Environmental Systems, Environmental Science, Technology and Social Change, Peace and Conflict Studies, Experimental Science, Philosophy, Geography, History, Math, and the Arts.

The IBO's stated mission is to build "intercultural understanding and respect" among "compassionate and lifelong learners who understand that other people, with their differences, can also be right."

Earth Charter

According to Education for a Free America, a watch group operating out of Chaska, Minnesota, the IBO teaches American children that UN resolutions are right and just, even when they are not approved of and they are sometimes damaging to the United States. Students are taught that the international resolutions passed by the UN outrank U.S. law as interpreted by the Supreme Court.

One example of teachings contrary to U.S. interests is the Earth Charter, a document not ratified by the United States that contains numerous provisions contrary to America's nature and interests, yet IBO students are taught to "embrace the spirit and aims of the document."

The Earth Charter says that capitalism is destroying the Earth by steadily depleting the planet's natural resources. The American way, it states, will "denude the Earth."

It advocates the redistribution of wealth from rich countries to poor countries, same-sex marriage, pantheistic spiritual education, military disarmament, and creation of an international agency that would make the Earth Charter binding on all nations.

Another Sermon on the Mount?

The charter calls for itself to be binding law that governs the world according to its own blatantly socialist ideology. When the charter was first written, Soviet Premier Mikhail Gorbachev bragged that his "hope is that this charter will be a kind of Ten Commandments, a 'Sermon on the Mount,' that provides a guide for human behavior toward the environment in the next century." Could the attempt to replace the Judaic-Christian tradition be any more obvious?

UNESCO also heaped on the praises, saying the charter was "undoubtedly one of the most powerful instruments for promoting the changes in our ways of life which must take place irrespective of any differences that may exist between us and which are driven principally by the imperative to conserve life on Earth."

According to the IBO's website, "The Global Teaching and Learning Project of the UN in New York accepted an IBO tender to produce two teaching booklets about UN global issues.... They will be copyrighted by the UN, with acknowledgement to the IBO for its work, and disseminated to the governments of all member states for use in school."

The committee that wrote the Earth Charter was led by Gorbachev. Another author was Maurice Strong, a Canadian, who was entangled in the UN's Oil-for-Food scandal, the subject of the chapter, "The Big Rip-Off: Oil for Food."

Ark of Hope?

The document, this "next Ten Commandments," was completed in 2001, and a party was held on September 9, just two days before the terrorist attacks on New York and Washington. The religious symbolism at that celebration was not subtle. To house the charter, a handcrafted chest called the Ark of Hope was built. Inside the ark was a papyrus copy of the charter, and on the outside were carved spiritual symbols, including unicorns, which were supposed to "ward off evil."

Many saw this ark as a mockery of Christianity and put it in the same category as the "new Commandments" and "new Sermon" comments out of Russia.

Two days later, when the World Trade towers fell and a hole was blasted in the side of the Pentagon, those behind the charter seemed largely unaffected by the fact that the unicorns hadn't done their job.

The Earth Charter remains the "Ten Commandments" of IBO, the book through which American children are indoctrinated into socialist thinking.

Brainwashing Techniques

One whistle-blowing IBO teacher had exposed the brainwashing techniques used at his IBO school in Kansas. The teacher said he used the Earth Charter for six years. During that time several hundred American students were exposed to it.

The teacher wrote, "Students use the Earth Charter in critical thinking/writing and discussion exercises. I also use it as part of the Ethics unit. After becoming familiar with the Earth Charter, students pick and choose principles that they are particularly interested in assimilating within projects and writings. Success and failure are directly related to student ability and interest. Students are adept at making connections from the Earth Charter to issues challenging their future across the board from social justice, environmental, democracy, and nonviolence issues."

The Earth Charter Initiative Secretariat laid out themes for lesson plans in a thick volume called the *Guidebook for Teachers*. Almost every lesson had to do with extreme environmentalism and wealth redistribution. The guidebook said students were to be taught to "recognize the importance of the environmental and social costs of goods and services." Students were told to ponder why "a small percentage of the population—the powerful—control a large percentage of the world's wealth."

The Earth Charter was indoctinating students as young as third graders. They were being taught that "fundamental changes in our patterns of production, consumption, and reproduction are needed in order to safeguard Earth's regenerative capacities, human rights, and community well-being."

The bottom line here was that third graders were being taught that it was in the best interests of the planet to replace capitalism with socialism and to halt population growth. In the IBO curriculum, opposing viewpoints went unheard.

Joseph A. Klein, author of *Global Deception: The UN's Stealth Assault on America's Freedom,* opined that the IBO schools in the United States should stop receiving U.S. tax dollars because the Earth Charter constitutes a religion, thus breaking our separation of church and state regulations.

Allen Quist, a three-time Minnesota state legislator and adjunct professor of political science at Bethany Lutheran College, concluded, "The foundational principles of the United States are summarized in the Declaration of Independence and are properly called the 'twelve pillars of freedom.' In addition to what IBO promotes, it rejects all twelve of these Declaration principles. Amendment Ten of our Bill of Rights clarifies that all the rights in our Bill of Rights are inherent and inalienable." Quist noted that IBO rejected the Bill of Rights tenth amendment, and therefore rejected the Bill of Rights in its entirety.

Fighting Back

It is important to note that not all boards of education across America have sat on their hands and allowed the UN to indoctrinate their children with anti-American notions.

On February 20, 2006, in Upper St. Clair, Pennsylvania, the board of education voted to eliminate the IBO program in their elementary, middle, and high schools. The given reason was that it was too expensive and benefited too few students, but behind the scenes, board members were deeply troubled by the one-world government bent of the curriculum.

The board held a public meeting on the subject, and many parents in the region voiced strong objections to the curriculum. They said a globalist philosophy was being pushed by UNESCO and IBO. The philosophy targeted children and urged increased UN power at the expense of national sovereignty.

Others in the Pennsylvania community strongly supported the IBO program, causing a ruckus that necessitated intervention from police and security officers. When the school board members voted to boot IBO out of their district, they received death threats from parents angry that their children no longer had access to the program. Predictably, the left-leaning American Civil Liberties Union (ACLU) complained about the action and threatened a lawsuit.

No surprise there either. The ACLU, which has long fought to keep the real Ten Commandments out of the classroom, was fighting to keep the Earth Charter, the new Ten Commandments, in.

UN Schemes to Tax Americans

There are plans at the UN, coming straight from the top, to eliminate the middleman and create a system whereby the UN could stick its hand directly into Americans' pockets. An unusually vocal attempt to make more efficient the money flow from the United States to the UN was openly discussed near the turn of the century by then UN secretary-general Kofi Annan.

(A quick aside: Our favorite Annan quote comes from February 24, 1998, when he was asked if he felt he could trust Saddam Hussein, the genocidal Iraqi dictator. Annan replied, "I feel I could do business with him." Maybe this wasn't the guy we wanted in charge of the UN.)

In 2000, the General Assembly approved a "Millennium Declaration" that would commit the world body and its member nations to five goals to be achieved by 2015. They aimed at reducing poverty, improving children's health, and fighting AIDS around the world.

In 2001, going with the flow, Annan was asserting a desire to "find new sources of funding" for the UN, when he said, "The need to finance the provision of global public goods in an increasingly globalized world also adds new urgency to the need for innovative new sources of financing."

Speaking at the World Economic Forum in Davos, Switzerland, Annan told the conference of the world's financial elite of a proposal by the UN Development Program (UNDP) to take seven trillion dollars from developed nations for use by the UN to assist the world's poorest nations.

A proposal for taxation on individuals in the richest countries, with the United States at the top of the list, was not new. Various plans had been embraced in academic circles and liberal and Socialist think tanks for decades. But while the United States and other developed nations historically prevented the UN from implementing the idea of direct taxation, increasing domination of the UN General Assembly by so-called developing nations resulted in revitalization of the quest to take and keep for themselves the wealth of citizens from nations like the United States through "redistribution."

In Davos, Annan claimed that unless development assistance was doubled to $100 billion annually, the world's 132 developing nations would not meet Millennium Development goals.

The CO_2 Tax

Using the Millennium Goals as the excuse, the UN began considering specific methods to extract wealth from citizens of the United States and other first-world nations. The one with the potential to garner the most money was a tax on gasoline, fuel oil, natural gas, and coal. Using global warming as an excuse, these taxes were meant to reduce the amount of greenhouse gases added to the atmosphere by the burning of fossil fuels.

Proponents argued that such a "carbon" tax would combat global warming by discouraging the use of fossil fuels, with the revenue from such a tax redistributed to poorer nations. One UN paper suggested that such a tax could yield $750 billion per year, with U.S. taxpayers stuck for more than $150 billion.

"UN Tax Grab"

Calling these ideas a "UN tax grab," Texas congressman Ron Paul warned, "UN bureaucrats think rich nations like America ought to give more money to poor nations—a lot more—simply because we're rich.

"Never mind the billions of foreign-aid tax dollars we send overseas every year; never mind the billions donated to overseas charities by Americans, the most charitable people on Earth.

"The UN mindset blames the Western world for poverty everywhere, assuming that our relative wealth must have come at the expense of the Third World. The poor countries themselves are never deemed responsible for their own predicaments, despite their often corrupt governments, lack of property rights, and hostility toward wealth-producing capitalism.

"Somehow, it's always our fault. So the UN holds conferences to talk about how we should pay to make things right, and the idea of a UN tax naturally arises," Paul concluded.

On August 17, 2004, the UN issued a seventeen-page report on "innovative sources of financing for development." The report, approved by Annan, made explicit references to global taxes and carried the endorsement of the UN General Assembly.

The UN also prepared a book titled *New Sources of Development Finance*, advocating global environmental taxes and a global currency tax that would affect the international investments of ordinary Americans.

In seeking a global tax, the UN demanded that the United States spend 0.7 percent of its gross national income on foreign aid. According to Jeffrey D. Sachs, Annan's special advisor, the U.S. was short by $65 billion each year. Over the thirteen-year period of time when the United States was expected to meet its own Millennium Development Goal, this amounted to $845 billion over and above what the United States spent on foreign aid. Sachs favored a global tax to force the United States to pay up.

A Penny a Megabyte

Global taxation zealots at the UN also envisioned a rich opportunity in the use of the Internet. Under their plan, e-mail users would pay a tax of about a penny for each megabyte of data that they sent, generating up to $150 billion a year.

While advocates admitted that such a tax might discourage use of e-mail, interfere with the least-regulated means of communication in the world economic marketplace, and be technically difficult to administer, they were unable to resist raiding what they saw as an untapped pot of gold. The tax, they said, would "raise funds that would be spent to narrow the 'digital divide' between rich and poor" nations.

Tobin Tax

Easier to collect would be a currency transaction tax (CTT) that would be imposed on nearly $300 trillion exchanged on open markets around the world by international banks, many of them U.S. based.

Called the Tobin Tax, it was proposed by Professor James Tobin of Yale University. The tax would generate up to $264 billion a year. Proponents also wanted the tax plan to mandate that the proceeds go into a global fund that "would redistribute tax revenue away from financial center countries in favor of low-income nations."

In order to make the tax more palatable, a UN paper suggested that the tax might start at an extremely low rate and increase over time. The CTT would raise the cost of nearly everything.

Opponents of the tax predicted the tax would hamper the free exchange of currency on world markets and possibly spawn a black market for money trading.

Fly Tax

A proposed international air transport tax would be levied on all international cargo and passenger flights to be paid by the airlines. Supporters of this scheme said that because air transport of passengers and cargo were a key source of environmental pollution, the tax would force the airlines and, ultimately, their passengers and shippers to pay for polluting the skies while providing money to the UN.

According to one estimate, an international transport tax would generate $2.2 billion per year. Though supporters conceded that the tax would have a harmful effect on tourism and the world economy at large, they claimed the benefits to the environment and the cash it generated outweighed those negative consequences.

Other Proposed Taxes

Very similar to the air transport tax, another plan would place a levy on airline fuel costs to the tune of about $12.5 billion per year.

Other UN tax proposals included the following:

- A tax on the international conventional arms trade
- A fine for ocean dumping
- A tax on commercial fishing
- A tax on Earth-orbiting satellites
- A tax on the use of the electronic spectrum (TV, radio, cell phones, etc.)
- A tax on the profits of international businesses
- A tax on advertising

While the names and proposals were different, the drive toward world taxation focused on three key purposes:

1. Making policy through high taxes on gasoline in order to reduce use of fossil fuels
2. Generating revenue for the UN
3. Redistributing income from the United States and other rich nations to the poorer ones in the Third World

Determined to oppose and block these goals, George W. Bush appointed a UN ambassador whose appearance in its hushed and hallowed halls was the equivalent of putting a fox in the hen house.

His name was John R. Bolton, and he proved to be a forceful advocate of American interests, a powerful voice for UN reform, and a staunch defender of the cause of human rights. We will learn about him in detail in the chapter titled "The Ambassador the UN Hated."

The Big Rip-off: Oil for Food

U.S. media, perhaps as a function of pack journalism (uniformity of news coverage), mostly *ignores* the anti-American bent of the UN. American news reports, be they in print or electronic, treat the UN as they always have, as a supranational organization dedicated to world peace.

For decades, the plastic talking heads and ink-drenched wretches of the media have bought the package. Some of the more investigatory among them may have learned the truth—but they didn't report it.

It was like the old adage often quoted by journalists over drinks, "Given the choice between the myth and the truth, write the myth every time." Going the other way was just trouble.

Breaking Away from the Pack

American conservatives were first to pick up on how the UN battered American interests at every turn. Foremost among the conservative outlets that called a spade a spade was Fox News, which frequently featured commentary that criticized the UN for biting the hand that fed them. The United States paid such a large portion of the UN's budget and all, they deserved to get a blankety-blank fair shake. Luckily for the First Amendment, there are still journalists and TV reporters who will break away from the pack.

Although the UN approved the action that drove Iraq out of Kuwait in 1990, it later failed to force Saddam Hussein to comply with sanctions. After authorizing the U.S. invasion in 2003, it turned against the Bush administration's war against Islamic terrorism.

Biggest Theft in History

UN officials pillaged the Iraq Oil-for-Food program and turned the humanitarian assistance plan into the biggest theft in history. The plan was both simple and ridiculous: Iraq could sell oil to the rest of the world in exchange for food and other necessities for the Iraqi poor. Guess how much money made it to the Iraqi poor?

That story of corruption in the Oil-for-Food system was broken by the award-winning journalist Claudia Rosett who wrote of the billions in UN funds intended for humanitarian relief inside Iraq ending up instead in the pockets of terrorists, politicians, and Saddam himself.

It was not uncommon for Saddam's treasury to be fattened with money that was intended for the Iraqi people, but when that money came out of U.S. wallets via a UN initiative, the news was shocking.

Soothing Angry Voices

The Oil-for-Food program took place between the wars in Iraq. The program was initiated by U.S. president Bill Clinton, who sought to soothe angry voices, decrying U.S. sanctions against Saddam's regime, claiming that they were unfairly cruel to Iraqi poor people.

Clinton's program went into effect in 1995 with UN resolution 986. Iraqi representatives signed a memorandum of understanding regarding the implementation of the program.

It was a new-and-improved version of an old Oil-for-Food resolution from 1991 that first allowed that exchange to be made. It remained in effect for eight years. The resolution was specific that none of the money offered in exchange for the Iraqi oil should go to the Iraqi military.

"Monthly Food Baskets"

About $65 billion dollars' worth of oil was sold by Iraq. According to the official books, two thirds of that money went to food and medicine, while the remainder went to rebuild Kuwait after its invasion by Iraq and subsequent liberation by the United States.

The program was not a favorite of the Pentagon. Did feeding Iraqi's poor have a solid tactical advantage? In a socio-economic way, maybe. Maybe the plan was to cut down on the cost of postvictory security by appeasing the unwashed masses now.

The Pentagon thought it was so long term as to be hooey. There was an immediate reason not to feed the poor. Iraqi hunger translated into social unrest, rendering Saddam easier to topple.

During the program's existence, the success of its efforts were wildly exaggerated by its UN executive director, Benon Sevan of Cyprus. He said that 90 percent of the Iraqi population was being fed through the program. That tremendous majority was reliant, he said, on the "monthly food baskets" the UN sent.

When the Oil-for-Food scandal broke, and an investigation commenced, Sevan was destined for arrest, but he fought mightily. He built a solid wall between himself and the evidence he allegedly had in his possession.

Sevan gave the authorities permission to do nothing and access to nothing. Court orders needed to be acquired. He knew he was fighting a losing battle, but nonetheless he fought tenaciously. As Sevan stalled the UN's internal investigator Dileep Nair, he used the bought time to shred more documents.

Annan Sings the Praises

As late as 2003 with Oil for Food in its last days, Annan was still singing the program's praises; singing loud and clear; and saying that it was the biggest, most complex, and unusual task ever undertaken by the Secretariat—and, with pride, Annan announced the Oil for Food had been a smashing success.

What a concept, he boasted: the only humanitarian program in the history of humankind to be funded exclusively with resources belonging to the nation it helped. Annan said that he had watched the program like a proud dad during its seven-plus years of operation.

In the early days, he said, the program faced "an almost impossible series of challenges," but it had overcome them. He was proud to say that $46 billion worth of Iraqi oil was sold in exchange for food and medicine for the impoverished citizens of Iraq.

The goods had been successfully distributed in twenty-four different regions across Iraq, regions chosen based on need. Annan said that there was still some money left and that it was going to go toward transferring power inside Iraq to the Coalition Provisional Authority (CPA). Happy days.

Oil for Food operated until the U.S. invasion of Iraq rendered the UN resolution null and void. At that point—with the U.S. president calling "mission accomplished"—the welfare of the Iraqi people, poor and otherwise, became the responsibility of the provisional government put in place to run Iraq after Saddam was ousted. At that point the UN was off the hook. A few very rich men were sorry to see the program terminate.

Eight Years of "In the Meantime"

In the meantime, you know what happened. Once the United States occupied Iraq, the abuses of the Oil-for-Food program became increasingly clear.

First of all, Saddam had taken personal control of the Oil-for-Food program. Everything the UN program sent to Iraq went where Saddam wanted it to go. If that was the case, it probably went into his own pocket. Who knew where it all went? Maybe some of it was bombed during the invasion, the rest to scavengers. It was gone. Your tax dollar at work.

The first public notice of impropriety in the program came in 2004. *Al Mada*, an Iraqi daily newspaper, published a list of Oil-for-Food contracts that had been in effect at the time of the invasion. Fifteen thousand pertinent documents were found in a now-occupied Iraqi oil refinery.

Kickbacks

In those reams of paper was evidence that, skipping the middleman, there were businessmen in Europe who were being allowed to buy oil directly through the Oil-for-Food program, at those *nice* and thrifty UN food-and-medicine prices.

The UN contracts, it was discovered, went to those willing to pay the kickback. Kickbacks were necessary to both buy oil and to sell food and medicine so the white-collar criminals leeched their victims coming and going.

The men involved in the scandal were wealthy European ambassador types, the sort of men who would, after cocktails, charter choppers to see their mistresses on their yachts.

Saddam, it would later be revealed, not only took a percentage of everything on the Iraq end but used the program in cunning ways, such as hammering a wedge between members of the Western powers by selling oil to some but not others. France, Russia, and China got contracts through the UN program. The United States and Great Britain did not.

Bad Banker

There were cunning crooks on the other end of the money trail as well. For the first six years of its existence, the Oil-for-Food program channeled its considerable budget through the BNP Paribas bank owned by Nadhmi Auchi, an Iraqi who for a time became the thirteenth richest man in England; then he received a fifteen-month suspended sentence for his involvement in Great Britain's biggest post–World War II fraud.

That case involved a bank and 200 million pounds in skimmed funds, the diverted money going to maintain a lavish ambassadorial lifestyle, including stunning investments in women and real estate. For years the busy but porous pipeline of UN billions ran through Auchi's bank.

House Committee Investigation

Once the stories of Oil-for-Food corruption commenced, the story grew. Congress got into the act. A U.S. House Committee on International Relations found that Auchi's bank made payments on behalf of the program, without verifying that the food and medicine were being delivered.

The House Committee investigation revealed that many, many checks were written by the program to persons or organizations that bank officials later could not verify as authorized program participants. Auchi's bank also accepted $700 million in *fees* from the UN account.

In its final report on the case, the House Committee concluded that at first the Oil-for-Food program had saved the Iraqi economy, which had been in a free fall due to economic sanctions. Iraq soon realized how easy Oil for Food would be to misappropriate. It used the stolen UN funds to strengthen Iraq's infrastructure and military capabilities.

Who Benefited Most?

The results of the House Committee investigation made the U.S. military seethe. The UN program made the invasion of Iraq more difficult by funding Iraq's military defenses. How stupid.

When the participants' involvement was monetarily quantified, Russia, France, and China were the largest Food-for-Oil benefactors, in that order. The United States wasn't even in the top ten and was categorized as "Other."

Not only was the system corrupt but designed to help them and not us. Very little of those U.S. tax dollars found their way back to the States, even in a corrupt fashion.

Volcker's Findings

As the scandal grew, the UN assigned its own investigatory team to the case. That crew predictably focused on the non-UN aspects of the corruption, although scapegoating one UN bigwig.

The head UN investigator, former Federal Reserve chairman Paul Volcker, released his final report on Oil for Food during the autumn of 2005. That report said the system's single largest source of kickbacks was the Australian Wheat Board, a supplier of food for the program.

Following that money trail, Volcker discovered checks sent to Iraqi companies to truck the food to their distribution points—companies that owned no trucks.

Even when the program got it right, it got it wrong. The food that did arrive at its designated target was spoiled in transit and unfit for consumption. A February 3, 2005, interim report by Volcker's commission announced that insufficient budget had been allocated to keep the food edible.

A large portion of the investigation focused on a top Oil-for-Food official. Evidence showed the official had taken $150,000 in bribes during his time near the administrative peak of the Oil-for-Food pyramid.

It was believed that that figure represented a small fraction of the money that the man had skimmed. He was fired by the UN, then arrested by Interpol. In 2007, the UN official was indicted in New York City for accepting bribes.

Lingering Stench

The stench from the Oil-for-Food case lingered in the world's court-rooms. In 2007 Germany was still busy prosecuting the white-collar criminals who had paid kickbacks to the UN program in exchange for cheap oil.

On January 6, 2006, a South Korean businessman was busted by the FBI in Houston, Texas, and charged with illegally accepting millions of dollars from Iraq during the Oil-for-Food program.

In October 2009 *Vanity Fair* reported that the Federal Reserve had shipped to Baghdad a total of $12 billion. Of that, less than a quarter was recovered, and the remainder had "gone missing, unaccounted for in a frenzy of mismanagement and greed."

Salvo of Lawsuits

As late as January 2010, Iraq's commerce minister Safaldin al-Safi announced to the world press that Iraq planned to file lawsuits in the United States against the foreign firms who defrauded Iraq during the Oil-for-Food program while Saddam was still in power.

Al-Safi said, "We have asked an American lawyer to prosecute the companies that violated the law regarding Oil-for-Food program." He refused to be more specific, although according to the French newspaper *Liberation*, one of the primary targets of the legal action was to be on the previously discussed BNP Paribas Bank.

Assessment of the Damage

So how much did Saddam make from the Oil-for-Food program? The job of tracing the money was the responsibility of the U.S. Government Accountability Office (GAO), as part of a larger study of Saddam and his safes full of American dollars. The money didn't end up doing Saddam any good in the end, that was for sure. Despite his riches, he was invaded, ousted, and executed.

The investigation concluded that during his regime, Saddam had obtained more than $10 billion in illegal revenues. About 60 percent of that was oil smuggling, the rest consisted of bribes and skims.

The GAO reported, "Both the UN secretary-general, through the Office of the Iraqi Program (OIP) and the Security Council, through its sanctions committee for Iraq, were responsible for overseeing the Oil-for-Food program. However, the Iraqi government negotiated contracts directly with purchasers of Iraqi oil and suppliers of commodities, which may have been one more important factor that allowed Iraq to levy illegal surcharges and commissions."

On the other end of the money pipeline, it was determined that 2,200 companies from more than forty different countries colluded to bilk the UN program.

Rape, Sex Slaves, and Pedophilia

W e should warn you up front. This chapter ain't pretty. In fact it's pretty doggone revolting, involving sexual *perversion*, *prostitution, and pedophilia*. UN employees have repeatedly been implicated in cases involving human smuggling, sex slaves, and child abuse in several poor countries around the world. So if you are sensitive to that type of material, skip to the next chapter. For the rest of you, here's the nightmare...

A Pre-Deluge Droplet

The first sex scandals to strike the UN were mild compared with those that would follow. In 1988 an American woman working in New York for an Argentinean diplomat who was the second-highest official in the UN Development Program (UNDP), accused her boss of raping her. Six years later the UN announced, in as small print as they could get away with, that the diplomat had ponied up $210,800 in damages and legal fees to make the case go away.

In 2004 UN inspectors investigated a sexual harassment complaint in Geneva, Switzerland, against the UN's high commissioner for refugees, Ruud Lubbers, a sixty-five-year-old legend who had once been prime minister of the Netherlands. Lubbers maintained his innocence through-out an investigation by the UN's Office of Internal Oversight Services.

Lubbers' accuser was a woman in her forties, employed by the UN for more than twenty years. She said that Lubbers grabbed her in an inappropriate way after a 2003 meeting in Lubbers' Geneva office. A judge threw the case out in 2008 ruling that Lubbers had diplomatic immunity from such charges.

But these incidents, if they contained any merit at all, were molehills compared to the mountainous sex scandals that were brewing for the UN in poor nations.

The reports eventually became so horrible and so frequent that the UN's propaganda machine was forced to address the uncomfortable issues. It included the subject of heinous sex crimes in poor nations as just one of many injustices it hoped to wipe out with its good vibes.

"Sex Slave/Child Combatant"

These things just happened, the UN said. It said more about the nature of war-torn areas than about the UN. A 2009 article on the official UN website, written by Radhika Coomaraswamy, pointed out the problems that children in war zones have, particularly girls.

This was true for child soldiers as well as civilian residents of "hot spots." There were young girls, the article said, whose job description was "sex slave/child combatant."

Some joined up because they were believers in the ideology, others were runaways out of options. The article detailed the story of one Columbian girl who ran away from an abusive father and followed her brothers into the military, where, in addition to fighting, she was expected to satiate the sexual needs, and improve the morale, of the men.

She described incidents, almost ceremonial, of being gang-raped in camp. Other attackers preferred privacy and waited until she was away from camp, gathering firewood, when the attacks came. Sadism and schematic misogyny were pervasive.

The prospects for a successful life once a girl found herself in this situation were slim. Those who were not killed in battle, or snuffed by abuse, were left emotionally and physically scarred. Unable to feel romance and to support themselves, they often turned to civilian prostitution.

The young girls of the war zone didn't have much of a shelf life. Often they were there one minute and then, poof they were gone—just disappeared off the planet. One disappeared here, another down the street, a third disappeared from over there.

When there was war, great flocks of children were stolen, taken away, smuggled, and sold—a slaughter of the innocents. Research had shown that human trafficking activity often came in waves and that these waves coincided with armed conflicts. War vultures swooped in after battles and hauled away the youngest and prettiest of the survivors.

"Our Own Peacekeepers..."

What was being done? A UN resolution (number 1612) was passed in 2005 creating a Working Group on Children and Armed Conflict. The Working Group reports once every other month on reports of trouble zones where human rights violations against children are most acute.

But the UN had a more complex problem when it came to the child sex trade. Some of the reports the Working Group was receiving were critically close to home.

An article written by the *UN Chronicle* said that the Working Group finally admitted that "the ground realities of conflict still lead to the sexual vulnerability of girls and women. Our own peacekeepers have not been immune to these situations."

UN Perverts

Say what? Sex crimes committed by UN peacekeepers? Well, yes. Many. Despite the hyperactivity of the UN's propaganda wing, the frequency and similitude of those reports were frightening. Sex abuse by UN reps was systemic, the norm.

The UN labored hard to prevent these types of situations in the future. When it came to dishing out the aid in war-torn regions, priority would be shown to orphans and households headed by a child. The UN was proud to proclaim that, with the addition of NGOs, it was serving as an advocate for war-displaced children, blah-blah-blah. In reality the UN was a player in the world's most profane and perverted sexual abuse of children.

Haiti, Three-Plus Years Before the Earthquake

During the autumn of 2006, the BBC reported on rape charges against UN employees in Haiti. The report said that peacekeepers had subjected Haitian children to rape and prostitution. Underage girls had sex with UN soldiers for money on a regular basis.

According to the BBC, a "high-ranking UN official" said the reports were "credible." Jane Holl Lute, the secretary-general for peacekeeping operations, confirmed for the BBC that the sexual abuse of children in Haiti was widespread and "we've had a problem probably since the inception of peacekeeping—problems of this kind of exploitation of vulnerable populations."

She now assumed in advance that whenever the UN began a new peacekeeping mission there would be a problem with the sexual exploitation of the region's minors.

Rape Outside the Palace

When the BBC looked into the situation in Haiti, they found an eleven-year-old girl who said she was sexually abused by UN peacekeepers outside the gates of the presidential palace in Port-au-Prince. The BBC also talked to a fourteen-year-old who described being abducted and raped inside a UN naval base in 2004.

As of November 2006, 316 peacekeeping personnel around the world were being or had been investigated for alleged sexual activity with children. Of those, reports showed, 18 civilians had been fired, while 161 military personnel were repatriated.

Culture of Silence

A representative of Refugees International said that the biggest obstacle facing investigations into these abuses was the "culture of silence" that existed in most military deployments.

And then a cry came from the disillusioned. The true believers out there, the aging hippies and showbiz people who still believed UN employees always wore a white cowboy hat, found the details of the UN's child sex crimes to be, to put it in their vernacular, a real mindblower.

But—but UN military deployments were supposed to be different. Those deployments were not composed merely of soldiers, but of men and women who were expected to be humanitarians as well.

You couldn't have more than three hundred offenders if the fear of punishment was sufficient. Fear of repatriation by the UN wasn't stopping the sex crimes. There needed to be legal ramifications for these abuses as well. Out of the three hundred or more incidents of UN employees and child sex, the Refugees International spokesperson said, there had been only two sent to jail.

Southern Sudan

In January 2007, the *London Telegraph* revealed that more than twenty different cases of child sex slavery involving UN staff members were reported in southern Sudan.

The victims, it was written, were as young as twelve. Dozens of victims claimed that some UN peacekeeping and civilian staff regularly picked up young children in their easily recognizable UN vehicles and forced them to have sex.

Hundreds of children may have been abused. The report stated that the abuses began in 2005 when the UN mission to southern Sudan (UNMIS) entered the region to help repair the damage done by twenty-three years of war there.

There were upward of ten thousand UN military personnel in the region from all nationalities—peacekeepers, military police, and civilian staff. The sex crimes commenced within weeks of the UN's arrival in southern Sudan. An internal UN memo was discovered by the *Telegraph* dated July 2005 that acknowledged there was a problem. During the course of its investigation, the London newspaper gathered accounts from twenty victims. The reports were all the same. Peacekeeping and civilian UN personnel were picking up children in their UN vehicles and raping them.

Jonas from Juba

Many of the stories came out of the city of Juba where there was a so-called lost generation of orphaned and abandoned children sleeping and surviving on the streets. A fourteen-year-old boy named Jonas in a *Telegraph* article said that he was sitting by the river the first time it happened. A man in a white car drove past and asked him if he wanted to get in the car with him.

"I saw that the car was a UN car because it was a white car with the black letters on it," Jonas said.

The boy recalled that the man showed him a badge, using his official status in an attempt to bully the youngster into compliance. The man was not requesting that the boy get in the car, he was ordering him to do so. The boy got in the car.

"When he stopped the car, he put a blindfold on me and started to abuse me," Jonas said. "It was painful and went on for a long time." When the sex act was completed, the boy was returned to the place where he had been picked up and released.

The saddest part of the story was the aftermath to the attack. One might assume that Jonas was frightened into hiding by the attack, but the opposite turned out to be the case.

Jonas told the British reporter that he frequently returned to the spot where he had been picked up by the man in the white car, in hopes that the man would partake of his sexual services again, this time in exchange for a much-needed fee. The man who attacked him did not return but the boy's sexual availability was noted by others, and he said he could make upward of three dollars a day selling himself to those who picked him up.

A Fistful of Cash

Other stories coming out of Juba were startlingly similar. A thirteen-year-old boy said he had been lured into a UN car by a man waving a fistful of cash, but the boy was later dumped out of the car without being paid.

If such an attack had taken place in the civilized world, the attack would have been verified by a medical examination, but that was out of the question in a region where there weren't enough doctors to take care of the sick and not enough certainly to cooperate with criminal investigations.

There were no criminal investigations. This was a lawless land. The streets were filled with innocent children, desperate for food and shelter and unprotected by law.

Konyo Konyo Square

The *Telegraph* reported that an unnamed NGO was investigating the allegations of UN sexual abuses in southern Sudan. This investigation was deemed necessary because the fledgling southern Sudanese government was too dependent on the UN to call out the organization for its employees' nasty habits.

The NGO study reported that sex crimes committed by UN personnel were "common" in the region. One of their sources was a twenty-three-year-old shoe shiner who worked in Juba's Konyo Konyo Square. From his location he saw much illicit activity and regularly saw UN-marked vehicles picking up and dropping off young girls, sometimes in groups, sometimes late at night. The report also said that the NGO investigator spoke to three girls, aged thirteen, sixteen, and eighteen, and all said that they'd had sex with UNMIS officials.

Ali Said, the Juba Judge

Perhaps the most damaging report came from Ali Said, a county court judge in Juba who said there had been a tremendous rise in child prostitution "since the UN arrived."

He said the "majority of people working for the UN are men and need to be entertained." Though the practices were common, criminal prosecutions for sex crimes in the region were nonexistent.

The reports served as strong psychological ammunition for the Sudanese government, a body that would love nothing more than for the UN to stay out of their business. Sudanese officials, it turned out, had conducted their own investigation into UN abuses and reportedly were in possession of photographs depicting UN peacekeepers, who happened to be from Bangladesh, having sex with three young girls.

Lute: "Lies!"

Jane Holl Lute said that reports from the Sudanese government shouldn't be taken as fact, unless confirmed by an outside source. Speaking to an American reporter from a news wire service, Lute said it was in the Sudanese government's best interests to make the UN look bad at every turn, so it couldn't automatically be believed.

What *could* be believed? Not much, according to Lute. "These environments are ones in which it is difficult to ascertain the truth," she said. "I do not believe these new allegations. Nevertheless we will treat them as seriously as we treat all other allegations."

She assured the concerned public that she had spoken to the head of the UN mission in southern Sudan, and he was aware of the UN policy regarding sex crimes and assured her that this policy would be implemented "across the board."

Lute added that if any allegations proved to be true, "we won't be complacent and there will be no impunity to the full extent of the UN's authority."

The "Few Bad Apples" Theory

The British regional coordinator of UNMIS, James Ellery, said that it was all a matter of numbers and probability. You had to take the reports of sex crimes in *context*.

Ten thousand was a lot of personnel, and given the size of that number and the many different nationalities and cultures that that number represented, there were bound to be a few "bad apples."

It didn't mean the UN was bad. And he wasn't even sure that there *were* a few bad apples. The reports he'd seen didn't seem reliable to him at all, and they were practically impossible to confirm.

None of the reports could even be traced back to a UN employee in particular. The eyewitness reports all featured men supposedly in UN vehicles. There was never an ID of an individual. There was certainly nothing that would stand up in a court of law or even before a UN disciplinary board. For all he knew, all the reports were part of a Sudanese conspiracy to drive the UN out.

He called Sudan the "most backward" country in all of Africa and said he wouldn't be surprised if these unsubstantiated reports were a backlash caused by a misconception as to the UN's role in the region.

Ellery may have tried to deflate the reports, but his superiors at the UN took matters far more seriously. The *Telegraph* investigative report prompted the UN to acknowledge the reports and announce that it was "launching an investigation."

The UN secretary-general Ban Ki-moon quickly noted that even as they became aware of this report out of Sudan, they were working harder than ever to help stop human rights violations in that region with the formation of a new peacekeeping mission.

The Ivory Coast

The UN's child sex problem was not limited to Sudan. In May 2008 a BBC report, based on a Save the Children investigation, said that children as young as eleven were subjected to rape and prostitution by UN peacekeepers in the Ivory Coast.

The charity proposed that an independent watchdog be set up in that area to prevent children from being abused by the very people who had been sent there to help look after them.

Save the Children noted that their own ranks were not immune to the problem and that three of their employees had been fired for breaching the organization's codes. The three men were fired for having sex with underage girls. All three performed their acts in regions where the activity was not a crime, but was against organizational rules.

Allegations against UN peacekeepers were plentiful, Save the Children reported. The report said that, despite this, child rape was unreported and unpunished because in the great majority of cases the diminutive victims were too frightened to report the attack. UN workers, the report said, had been abusing both young girls and boys.

Elizabeth, Thirteen

The Save the Children report included the story of a thirteen-year-old girl named Elizabeth in the Ivory Coast who claimed that she was gang-raped by ten UN peacekeepers in a field near her home.

The girl said, "They grabbed me and threw me to the ground, and they forced themselves on me. I tried to escape, but there were ten of them and I could do nothing. I was terrified. They just left me there bleeding."

According to Save the Children's Ivory Coast country director, Heather Kerr, little was being done to bring the UN peacekeepers to justice. Even less was being done to support the victims.

She said a minority of UN personnel were taking part in the attacks, it was true, but it was impossible to estimate how widespread the attacks were because the UN peacekeepers hold all the power and the children have no way to complain formally.

"They are suffering sexual exploitation and abuse in silence," Kerr said.

UN spokesperson Nick Birnback gave the BBC his version of the bad apples theory, stating that 200,000 people were employed by the UN around the world, so you couldn't assume they were all benevolent souls. Zero incidents, he said, was an unreasonable expectation.

"What we can do," he said, "is get across the message of zero tolerance, which for us means zero complacency when credible allegations are raised and zero impunity when we find that there has been malfeasance that's occurred."

Democratic Republic of the Congo

In December 2004 the *London Times* reported that a UN logistics expert in the Democratic Republic of the Congo was a child pornographer, and a juicy scandal ensued.

The video maker was French and worked out of the Goma airport as part of the UN's $700 million rebuilding package in that war-torn Central African nation.

After learning of the man's showbiz efforts, local police raided his house and found he had transformed his bedroom into a studio to videotape and photograph young Congolese girls in sexual situations.

There were mirrors covering three walls. Along the fourth wall was a mounted camera, set up so that it could be operated by remote control from the bed. When the police raided, the man was about to rape a twelve-year-old girl. The girl, who turned out to be a police plant, was rescued just in time.

Both Director and Costar

That police would use a twelve-year-old girl as bait for a rapist was upsetting enough, but it was secondary to the disturbing police discovery in the UN logistics expert's bachelor pad: three porn movies and fifty photographs, all depicting the most disgusting imaginable child abuse.

The UN sent the photographer, who also sometimes costarred in his videos, back to France where he was put in jail and charged with having sex with a minor.

Was it a fluke that the child pornographer arrested in this case worked for the UN? Hardly. There were 11,000 UN peacekeepers and one thousand civilians in the Congo. According to the *Times*, there was "apparently rampant sexual exploitation of Congolese girls and women."

Bunia Hotbed

It was understood that the number of complaints in the Congo about UN employees and young Congolese girls was a mere fraction of the probable total number of attacks.

Still, there were *150 allegations* of sexual misconduct against UN peacekeepers. The city of Bunia was a hotbed of pedophilia, as 68 of those allegations came from that city alone.

The UN's priority at the time of the child pornographer's arrest was not to paint the story in a light that made the UN look good, but to scour the Congolese world of pornography to prevent possible copies of the UN videos from going on sale.

No matter how bad the scandal was, it would be much easier to survive if no videos of the UN employee having sex with a child surfaced on the Internet. That mission was apparently successful as no photos or videos surfaced, but there remained the possibility that the obscene material had fallen into the hands of a private collector, one not above using it to blackmail the UN.

Paid in Mayonnaise and Jam

The *Times* unearthed some of the details among those 150 cases. Two UN pilots from Russia and based in Mbandaka, a city on the Congo River, were said to have paid young girls for sex. The price: jars of mayonnaise and jam.

These sex sessions were videotaped and those tapes were mailed to Russia. When UN investigators came to question the UN pilots, the pornographers were tipped off and successfully fled.

There were also multiple reports of hideous sex abuse from the Moroccan peacekeeping contingent in Kisangani, a town along the Congo River, inaccessible by road. The most unusual scenario coming out of that contingent was the one about the young soldier, accused of rape, who was hidden somewhere in the barracks from UN investigators for a year.

At Least 140 UN Pregnancies

The UN and pedophilia were synonymous in Central Africa due to the plentiful allegations. The most damaging quote of all came in 2002 from the rebel commander Major-General Pierre Ondekane who told a UN official that the only thing the UN Mission in the Congo would be remembered for was "running after little girls."

An NGO performed an investigation into the connection between the child sex trade in the Congo and the UN. It discovered more than 140 women and girls were impregnated by UN employees in that nation.

Of those, 82 were caused by the Moroccans in Kisangani. UN insiders told the *Times* that at least two UN officials were expelled from Congo for impregnating local women.

It was learned that the price for a child prostitute in the Congo was somewhere between one and three dollars. Or as frequently happened, the child was paid in food.

Rape Disguised as Prostitution

A technique used by the abusers was rape disguised as prostitution. UN employees raped the children and then gave them money to make it look like the victim had hustled for or otherwise instigated the sex and the income. What could the UN say? Not much.

"The fact that these things happened is a blot on us," the UN's under secretary-general of peacekeeping Jean-Marie Guéhenno said. He said there was nothing to do but make sure the guilty were punished.

UN spinmasters noted that the UN stubbornly clung to a higher moral code. Its rule was that their employees were to have no sex with anyone under eighteen years of age, despite the fact that in the Congo the age of consent was fourteen.

Security Threat

Lost amid the sordidness of the subject matter was the threat to security presented by the pervasive interweaving of UN and pedophiliac activities. Young prostitutes told UN investigators that they had no trouble getting into UN barracks, and it was safe to say that at least some of the abusers spoke freely around their diminutive victims.

"The guys on duty at the entrance know why we have come," one diminutive informant said. She once caught her UN "boyfriend" having sex with an even younger girl, perhaps ten. She was disgusted.

As one female UN employee in the Congo told the *Times* reporter,

"Never forget, this is *Heart of Darkness* country. People do things here because they can." *Heart of Darkness* was a novel by Joseph Conrad about widespread sociopathic behavior in the former Belgian Congo.

Kosovo Trafficking

In a 2004 Amnesty International report, it was revealed that both UN and NATO troops in Kosovo were frequently having sex with girls as young as eleven in exchange for looking the other way regarding the human trafficking business that thrived in that region. There were also reports that, at least in some cases, the UN operation was involved in the trafficking itself.

Amnesty International said UN peacekeepers in Kosovo were "fuelling the sexual exploitation of women and encouraging trafficking."

Amnesty International's UK director Kate Allen added that young girls from Eastern European countries were being sold into sex slavery. It was "time for countries to stop treating human trafficking as a form of 'illegal migration' and see it as a particularly vicious form of human rights abuse."

Sex Business Booming

Amnesty International interviewed women involved and discovered how these operations worked. The interviewed women were from Moldova, Bulgaria, and Ukraine and were brought to Kosovo to service Kosovo's booming sex industry.

The girls and women said they were smuggled across national borders and sold in "trading houses." They were "drugged and broken in." Buying a girl cost a customer anywhere between the equivalent of $60 and $4,200. The females were abducted, imprisoned, mistreated, and tortured, both physically and psychologically.

One woman told Amnesty International, "I was forced by the boss to serve international soldiers and police officers. I never had a chance of running away and leaving that miserable life because I was observed every moment by a woman."

Amnesty International also noted that the local law was less than helpful when it came to stopping the abuses. Despite the fact that the young women were clearly victims in this operation, when the law did come down, it came down on the girls, who were arrested and charged with prostitution.

The burgeoning sex industry really blossomed at the end of the twentieth century when 40,000 UN and other peacekeeping personnel entered Kosovo. In 1999 there were approximately eighteen bars, hotels, and nightclubs in Kosovo where prostitutes were available. By 2003 there were more than two hundred locations.

The Amnesty International exposé forced the UN to look at its own role in the sex business in Kosovo. Amnesty International later reported that by the summer of 2003, ten UN personnel had been fired or repatriated because of involvement with human trafficking.

The UN personnel were immune from prosecution in Kosovo. According to Allen, "The international community in Kosovo is now adding insult to injury by securing immunity from prosecution for its personnel and apparently hushing up their shameful part in the abuse of trafficked women and girls."

Liberia

During the spring of 2006, the BBC reported that the UN employees in charge of giving out the food and supplies for the UN mission in Liberia were demanding sex from girls as young as eight.

The BBC report included vivid, emotional photos and video footage. It was the same old story. There were torrents of refugees, and—as always seemed to happen in this situation—the cruelest were abusing the weakest.

When the BBC report was first aired, the UN announced an immediate investigation into "specific allegations." The systemic nature of the abuses in Liberia by UN personnel was beyond investigation. The crimes formed a pattern so unthinkable in civilized society that no one would believe it no matter how complete and reliable the evidence became.

A Picture Too Big to See

The UN investigatory "force" promised to take it alleged rape by alleged rape, and they wouldn't stop digging until they discovered the facts. But those investigators wouldn't spend a nanosecond contemplating the Big Picture.

What did it mean that so many UN employees were committing acts abhorrent to the civilized world? There would be no discussion of the Big Picture. The Big Picture was precisely what the UN was trying to cover up.

Luckily for the world's truth seekers, Save the Children also investigated sex abuse in Liberia, and they took a closer look at UN sex abuses than the UN investigators ever would.

Save the Children interviewed more than three hundred refugees in camps. They learned that the problem was "widespread." There were those people handing out the food who were sadistic pedophiles and used their power to acquire sexual favors from Liberian children.

Asked how many of the girls they knew had been the victim of sex abuse, the most common answer was "more than half." They called it "man business." There were slave markets where girls from eight to eighteen were bought and sold.

A BBC news crew entered refugee camps and questioned Liberian girls and young women. A twenty-year-old woman said that when she was younger she'd been forced to have sex with the guy in charge of the food distribution in her camp.

She said, "The young man was doing it to most of my friends. And the children, too, don't have strong minds. They will have sex with him to get the food."

East Timor

In 2003 the Associated Press reported that UN officials were identified as using a ship chartered for peacekeepers to traffic young girls from Thailand to East Timor as prostitutes. That identification was made by a former UN employee turned whistle-blower.

The details of the allegations were that often underage women were being trafficked from Thailand and other Asian countries to East Timor where they were forced to work in brothels as sex slaves. UN officers, the whistle-blower said, were often customers at the brothels and had sex with extremely young girls.

That spring a squad from the UN police force (UNPOL) raided a brothel called "Hava Fitness Thai Massage Parlor" in Dili, East Timor. To their horror, along with twenty-three Thai girls and women, they found six UNPOL officers taking care of "man business."

The men, desperately grabbing for towels, stammered that they were shocked. They had no idea that the joint was an illegal brothel and were just there to get a massage.

King's Naïvete

Alan King, East Timor's acting deputy operations commissioner in the UN mission, said that UNPOL was trying to shut down as many brothels as possible and denied there was a widespread human trafficking problem in the region.

The problem, King told an Australian television show, was massage parlors. They were very popular in East Timor and most were perfectly legitimate. But a few were *covers* for brothels, and those were the ones being raided.

King's naïve attitude encouraged UN complacency. Predictably in East Timor the problem only grew.

Freeway for Human Traffic

By 2009 organized crime had a firm grip on the brothels and the traf-ficking of fresh women from Thailand, Indonesia, China, and the Philip-pines. Traffic on this freeway flowed freely, unhindered by anyone's law.

An Australian reporter called the East Timor courts "dysfunctional" and noted that not a single conviction on charges of people trafficking had ever been recorded.

UN and East Timor police made arrests, but no one was ever found guilty. The reporter noted that while Dili's sex industry was nowhere near the size of that in Bangkok or Jakarta, it was entrenched and would be dif-ficult to dig out.

The pipeline that once only pumped women from Southeast Asia to East Timor now flowed both ways, with East Timor girls being abducted and taken to centers of illicit activity far away.

One projected difficulty with any proposed police action against human trafficking in East Timor was the lack of current security along the East Timor-West Timor border. Security provided by customs and immi-gration officials along that border was porous at best, and smugglers eas-ily moved girls across the line.

Sierra Leone and New Guinea Too

In early 2002 a massive pedophilia scandal within the UN was uncov-ered involving sexual abuse against West African refugee children in Sierra Leone and Guinea.

United Press International (UPI) reported that senior UN officials knew of the widespread pedophilia. Those same officials took no action against the perpetrators and instead worked to cover up the atrocities.

So does the UN plan to do anything about its employees regularly par-taking in egregious sex acts? They say yes. The UN's Department of Peacekeeping Operations says it is a priority to stop sex crimes committed by UN peacekeepers. This was important, the UN representative noted, so that representatives of the UN, whether they be diplomats or police, be seen universally as the good guys.

Good luck with that.

The Beat Goes On...

The UN already had built a well-deserved reputation as a "perved-out" organization, when the devastating Haitian earthquake of January 2010 struck. Even as the United States rushed to Haiti's aid, a forty-four-year-old former chief UN weapons inspector named Scott Ritter was arrested in Monroe County, Pennsylvania, caught in an antipedophilia sting operation.

The Pocono *Record* reported that in 2009, Ritter had allegedly exchanged obscene e-mail messages with undercover police officer Ryan Venneman who was pretending to be a fifteen-year-old girl named Emily.

Using the screen name "delmarm4fun," Ritter sent e-mails from his home in Delmar, New York, an Albany suburb. During his e-mail exchange with the undercover agent, Ritter allegedly asked Emily for her photograph, linked up a Web camera, and committed an act of autoeroticism.

Repeat Offender

Emily asked for his cell number. The number he provided allowed police to identify the man and make the arrest. Following Ritter's arrest, the *New York Times* looked into his background and discovered that Ritter had been in trouble before.

In 2001, Ritter had been caught in another law enforcement sting operation. On that occasion Ritter was accused of trying to lure a sixteen-year-old girl to an upstate New York fast-food restaurant. Charges against

Ritter in the 2001 case were dropped, provided that Ritter kept his nose clean.

Ritter's stint with the UN, from 1991 to 1998, was tumultuous. He was the chief weapons inspector for the United Nations Special Commission. During that time, he was a blunt-speaking critic of U.S. foreign policy in the Middle East and eventually resigned from his UN post.

And so we submit the case of Scott Ritter who proved that UN employees past and present did not have to be in a remote war-torn part of the world to appease their dark pedophiliac urges.

Nest of Thieves

The World Meteorological Organization (WMO) is, by its own definition, a specialized agency of the UN. It is the "UN system's authoritative voice on the state and behavior of the Earth's atmosphere, its interaction with the oceans, the climate it produces, and the resulting distribution of water resources."

As of 2009 it had a membership of 189 member states and territories. It was established in 1950, although in reality it evolved from the International Meteorological Organization (IMO) that had been around since 1873. The UN boasts that the WMO had played "a unique and powerful role in contributing to the safety and welfare of humanity." What the UN won't tell you is that it is also a nest of thieves, where everything top to bottom is fixed.

Financial Irregularities

According to the *International Herald Tribune*, the 2003 election of the WMO chief was certainly fixed. Government delegates received bribes in order to vote for the eventual winner.

The story, originally reported by the AP, was based on the statements of Maria Veiga of Portugal. The WMO, perhaps to its chagrin, had hired Veiga as an independent auditor in search of financial irregularities, and she'd done her job well. Too well.

Predictably, after reporting on the irregularities she uncovered, she was fired because of "gross misconduct." A tactical error on the WMO's part. Veiga was now a disgruntled ex-employee, eager to retaliate against the organization—the corrupt organization—that had wronged her.

Skims and Bribes

The angry whistle-blower told her story to a reporter. Before she was fired, she said, she was warned to stop her investigation. She was threatened when she did not.

Veiga gave the reporter a sixty-five-page summary of her investigation's findings. She charged that a former WMO staffer, Muhammad Hassan of Sudan, skimmed $3 million from the WMO while working in its training department. That $3 million, Veiga's report asserted, was used to bribe the voters in the 2003 WMO election.

It was used to pay for travel, accommodations, and the pocket money of delegates of certain countries in the WMO with the understanding that the delegates would then vote according to Hassan's wishes.

The WMO protested the allegations. Not the part about the money being skimmed—that was to be expected. Delegates were bound to have personal enrichment as a motive; it was only human nature. But that stuff about fixing the election, that was all hooey, the WMO said.

Tsunami Bribes

This den of thieves rears its corrupt head even in the face of disasters of biblical proportions, such as the tsunami in South Asia. While the great majority of humans responded generously and selflessly to the crisis, it was business as usual at the UN.

The UN had every reason to play this one straight, to provide a clean and open pipeline for the funds to reach the needy. The timing was such that it was still stinging from the Oil-for-Food scandal.

It was reported that money designated for the tsunami relief region was meeting the same fate as the money that had been pumped everywhere else. Contributors, hearing of the corruption, halted the flow of money.

Who picked up the slack? The U.S. government, that's who.

Bush Coalition

When George W. Bush announced that he was setting up a coalition of his own to deliver relief to the Asian disaster area, one might think that the UN would appreciate the help. Instead, the UN saw Bush's coalition as a rival.

Bush's team consisted of the United States, Japan, India, and Australia. His relief initiative brought a clipped response from former International Development secretary Clare Short.

"That role should be left to the UN," Short said. "I think this initiative from America to set up four countries claiming to coordinate sounds like yet another attempt to undermine the UN when it is the best system we have got and the one that needs building up. Only really the UN can do that job," Short told the BBC. "It is the only body that has the moral authority. But it can only do it well if it is backed up by the authority of the great powers."

Taking a dig at a slow response to the disaster along the Gulf of Mexico following Hurricane Katrina, Short criticized the record of the U.S. coalition for not having impressive records when it came to responding to disasters, international or otherwise.

She said the United States was "very bad at coordinating with anyone. I don't know what that is about, but it sounds very much, I am afraid, like the United States is trying to have a separate operation and not work with the rest of the world through the UN system."

Fear Mongers

The WMO continued to work hardest to keep the money flowing freely, the money from which corrupt forces within the WMO would skim and skim again.

The key to raising money was to spread fear. The WMO focused its fund-raising campaigns around climate change. It was very effective at getting its message across and could tub-thump with the very best of the fear mongers.

At the end of 2009, the WMO revealed the results of a huge study of world weather patterns over time. They determined that 2009 was the fifth hottest year since records were first kept in 1850. More troubling, the WMO added, was the past decade, the first of the twenty-first century, as it was the hottest ever recorded. More about the "global warming" campaign for funds in the chapter "Global Warming: The Big Lie." Because of all of this very important work, the WMO was going to need more money than ever.

Corruption in 2010

Nothing has changed. In 2010 a Florida businessman became embroiled in a legal maelstrom brought about by his own penchant for bribery. He was a former vice president for international sales for a major military and law enforcement equipment manufacturer and was adept at winning big-time contracts through bribery.

He was so good at it that he went undercover for the cops to help pull off a foreign bribery sting with twelve arrests. Then he played the same game again—only this time for real.

In January 2010 the businessman was busted for paying bribes to UN contacts from 2001 to 2006 in exchange for contracts to supply helmets, armored vests, pepper spray, and other protective gear to UN peacekeeping forces.

Individual Number One

The Florida businessman's days as an undercover operative for his country were through. There would be no more undercover work regardless of the client. The Justice Department fully outed him as "Individual Number One" who had been a "key intermediary" for the earlier twelve-bust sting.

That sting, documents revealed, had been put together by the FBI and had nailed a dozen individuals who, like Individual Number One, were manufacturers of military equipment. One made the introductions and posed as a broker for the bribes.

The poor saps. One's competition, ha! He set the trap perfectly, introducing the men to undercover agents, posing as representatives of an African nation. The case was noteworthy because it was the first to be prosecuted under the new Foreign Corrupt Practices Act, which specifically prohibited bribing foreign officials.

No Favors for Services Rendered

Individual Number One felt he had the right to some goodwill from the Feds for the big favor he'd done going undercover on their behalf—but no. Next thing he knew, he was under investigation himself. The Feds knew no gratitude.

According to court filings, the UN bribery scheme got under way in 2001 and involved Individual Number One and four others—three businessmen and a UN agent.

The subjects of the investigation allegedly conspired to bribe the UN officials in exchange for huge military contracts and export licenses. And they'd allegedly fudged the books to obscure the bribes—another crime.

In detail, there was intrigue with a few James Bond moments. The bribe for the $2.4 million pepper spray contract didn't come in the form of money but rather as confidential information.

Also of note was that from 2004 to 2008, Individual Number One was married to a prominent foreign policy specialist in the Clinton administration who served as a senior representative to the U.S. mission to the UN from 1997 to 2001. The wife's UN career as a diplomat, however, ended before any of the allegations against her then husband occurred.

Kosovo Bribes

Just as it was in Africa, Asia, and the Caribbean, the UN's operations in Europe during the 1990s—specifically, efforts in the war-torn region formerly known as Yugoslavia—were every bit as corrupt and inefficient.

Though the U.S. focus hasn't been on that region since 9/11, there is still unrest in that region, and UN corruption continues. On July 8, 2007, a representative of the Kosovo Liberation Army warned the International community (and the UN, in particular) to keep its corrupt hands off its business.

He then accused the UN Special Envoy for Kosovo, the former Finnish president Martti Ahtisaari, of taking bribes from the Albanian mafia in exchange for his support of independence for Kosovo.

On February 17, 2008, Kosovo declared its independence from Serbia. A year later it was recognized as an independent nation by its neighbor the Maldives. As of January, 2010, sixty-five of the 192 UN member states recognized Kosovo. So if the allegations were true, for the Albanian mafia it was money well spent.

Congo Gold

In November 2009 the CBS program *60 Minutes* dedicated an episode to the ways in which the global gold industry was fueling the anarchy and violence in the Congo. The many bands of militia in that country are warring with one another over turf—that turf being the region's lucrative gold deposits.

The unrest hadn't gotten a lot of play stateside, but it was huge. And an estimated five million people had met a violent end there, making it the most deadly war since World War II—and all because every faction wants all the gold.

So what did the UN peacekeeping forces do when they arrived in the Congo. They commenced messing around with the gold trade, of course. During the spring of 2007, Reuters reported that UN peacekeepers from Pakistan were trafficking arms for gold with one of the militia factions in the Democratic Republic of the Congo. In addition, UN cover-up artists were hindering inquiries into the charges.

The UN denied that any arms were given to the Congo militia. Pakistan called the accusations lies. There were 17,000 UN peacekeepers in the Congo, and that force, as we've seen, was already feeling embattled because of charges regarding human trafficking and pedophilia.

The new charges allegedly stemmed from late 2005 when Pakistani peacekeepers were stationed in the eastern Ituri district where there was still much fighting (in a war that was supposed to have ended two years before).

Anneke Van Woudenberg, senior researcher at the American firm of Human Rights Watch, told a Reuters reporter that between two and five million dollars' worth of gold was smuggled out of Ituri by Pakistani UN officers who were engaged in illegal smuggling. The group of smugglers mixed the UN officers with Indian businessmen and members of the local militia into a cohesive group of lawbreakers, Van Woudenberg added.

And so we can see the pattern. There is no such thing as legitimate UN business, there are only excuses to commit white-collar crimes in the form of embezzlement, blackmail, smuggling, and fraud.

One-World Government

L et's now take a closer look at the UN's attempt to eliminate the current system of sovereign nations and replace it with a global governor. For a couple of generations now, the UN has sought to transform itself into a world government capable of diminishing the power of Western democracies and promoting the growth of socialism and nondemocratic government.

The UN, in a primary sense, has dedicated itself to an un-American cause. The plan, apparently, is to become a dry sponge, soak up as much wealth from the United States as possible, and, when saturated, move to the Third World and squeeze.

The world's nondemocracies, some of which need American money more than others, want to give the UN real teeth, to empower the organization with legally binding international law. There would be nothing the UN couldn't do, once it was illegal to disobey.

The Organization of the Islamic Conference

In 2010, the largest and most frightening bloc of nondemocratic nations in the UN was the Organization of Islamic Conference (OIC), which consisted of fifty-seven countries that always, always vote together. Regarding Israel or Islam or matters of the troubled Middle East, the

OIC always had its way. As jihadwatch.org puts it, the OIC "calls the tune."

Amazingly, matters of the Middle East took up an estimated half of the UN's time, more time than world poverty and climate change combined. A third of the time was spent discussing the topic of Palestine. And it was while discussing Israelis and Palestinians that the language of the UN became most contentious.

On one side Israel was glorified, discussed in rhetoric suggesting an empire more than a nation. On the other Israel was described as a thorn in the world's side, a thorn that needed to be removed and destroyed to prevent a potentially fatal infection.

By 2009 the OIC had already gained control of the UN Human Rights Council and had infested the statements and rulings of the council with pro-Islam and anti-Western slogans. The OIC questioned Israel's right to exist and used the council as a political shield to hide its own soul-destroying human rights violations from the rest of the world.

Dogmatic Denouncements

Although there were voices of sanity on the human rights council, they were often obscured and then buried by the OIC's dogmatic denouncements, words that to Westerners sounded bizarre and crazy.

As a result, the well-thought-out ideas and concepts of great Western minds were often dismissed as evil and replaced by Islamic dogma. Everything was drastically simplified for the Arabic world, rendered polar by Islam itself.

Islamic ideology was all-encompassing and left no room for compromise. It was an ideology made up of blacks and whites, while both Far Eastern and Western minds grappled with the complexities of existence and the shades of gray that lay between. Islam taught obedience and stifled curiosity, encouraged worship and squelched imagination. It was an ideology that along its lunatic fringe had created global terrorism everywhere from New York City to Indonesia—with England, Pakistan, the Philippines, Kashmir, and the Balkans in between.

Beware the Lies Told by Western Arrogance

The Western mind, with all of its imagination, curiosity, and ambition, is nonetheless an arrogant entity—too quick to underestimate Islam. The assumption that their UN representatives are simple is in itself naïve, as it understates the matter.

It ignores the possibility that there is often the cunning of deception in the words of the bloc. Though they maintain with every breath that their power comes from God, outsiders can't help but suspect that deep down inside, they understand that their power comes from oil.

The Islamic countries cry louder each year that they deserve a seat on the Security Council and should have the veto power that is enjoyed by Security Council members. They boldly accuse the United States of abusing its veto rights in order to protect Israel.

Law of the Sea Convention

Another UN attempt to form a global government, a leftist New World Order, came with its efforts to regulate strictly for all nations the happenings above, on, and in the world's oceans.

The United Nations Convention on the Law of the Sea (UNCLOS) met from 1973 to 1982 and ultimately gave the world a treaty signed by representatives of sixty nations. They made laws that were applicable to *everyone*. Worse, the laws codified in the UNCLOS treaty didn't play fair. As usual, the United States and its allies were screwed.

The UN used cutout organizations to form a buffer between the UN and UNCLOS. These organizations were the International Maritime Organization, the International Whaling Commission, and the International Seabed Authority (ISA), NGOs that would implement and enforce the new Law of the Sea Treaty. The ISA was UN created, making the connection between the UN and the implementation of ocean law that much cozier.

Freedom of the Seas

For hundreds of years, there was no need for a book of maritime regulations. The law was simply put that there was freedom of the seas. Nations had rights to the waters three miles off their shore, the distance that could theoretically be covered by a cannon ball and everything else was international waters, available to everyone and belonging to no one.

By the twentieth century, the freedom of the seas rule was becoming increasingly inadequate. The world was rapidly growing more intricate. New problems were born. Increased pollution, improved mass fishing methods, and increased harvesting of sizable mineral deposits in formerly international waters were all matters that demanded regulation.

New Oceans Limits

The first attempt to regulate maritime behavior, to deny some of the freedoms of the sea, came in 1930 when the League of Nations met in The Hague to discuss it. No treaty was made, however.

In 1945, Truman simply announced that the United States no longer recognized the three-mile limit. The United States claimed for itself all of North America's continental shelf. A few years later, several South American countries extended their national waters as well to take better advantage of the Humboldt Current fishing grounds. Other countries with shorelines spoke up then, and the line for international waters extended from three to twelve miles.

Lose the Law of the Sea Treaty

The UN's Law of the Sea Treaty (LOST) was originally signed in 1982, but was determined to be too anti-American by Reagan. The treaty was revised (not enough) and was signed by Clinton.

The second Bush administration also said nice things about LOST, but it wasn't persistent once the opposition pushed back. However, the Obama administration worked toward a first time ever full ratification of the LOST treaty by the United States.

The ratification would make the United States directly responsible for funding the implementation and enforcement of LOST whether the laws benefited the United States or not. Mostly not.

Other Problems

The new laws not only unbalanced the playing field but stacked the deck against the Free World. Some of the laws were quick to anger red-blooded Americans. For one thing, looking at the big picture, it placed 70 percent of the world's surface under UN control.

Intolerable!

The UN's cutout, the ISA, would control the minerals and other natural resources of the ocean's bed. Any money made from these resources would be put directly into the UN's money pipeline, plagued by corruption, and headed for the anti-American zealots of Third World countries.

Why would the United States ever want to ratify this treaty? It had to do with the North Pole. Not ratifying would mean missing out on the only recently accessible Arctic resources.

But the trade still wouldn't be worth it. If the United States ratified, environmental organizations would gain the power to sue the U.S. government over just about anything, further draining us of cash. The whole thing is just another excuse to dip into Uncle Sam's pockets.

Stare Down with the Chinese

Although the United States still did not recognize LOST as of 2010, many other nations did, including world powers. This recognition became all too obvious during the second Bush administration when a U.S. military ship in the South Sea got into a stare down with a Chinese ship.

The Americans claimed the Chinese ship was "harassing" them. The Chinese said that the U.S. ship was in violation of LOST regulations and was therefore illegal.

The Chinese claimed that LOST gave them territorial rights to all waters within two hundred miles of their shore. Here was perhaps the biggest reason not to ratify LOST. If the United States climbed aboard this nonsense, commercial, military, and military intelligence operations on the high seas would be prohibitively restricted.

Global Courts

If you're going to have global laws, so goes the UN's theory, you're going to need global courts. Chapter XIV of the UN Charter established the International Court of Justice (ICJ) as the UN's judicial organ. That body was headquartered in a building known as The Peace Palace in The Hague. That same chapter authorized the UN Security Council to enforce World Court rulings.

The UN court is not the same as the International Criminal Court. It is designed to settle legal disputes between member states and to interpret international law at the behest of the UN General Assembly and a variety of UN satellite organizations. The five permanent members of the UN Security Council each has veto power over the court's decisions.

During the Reagan administration, the United States withdrew from the court's compulsory jurisdiction. Since 1986, the United States has only recognized the UN's court as real on a case-by-case basis.

The UN's court was criticized over the years for its lack of power. It could only be used when a dispute was between two UN member states. If an outsider was involved, the case was bumped up to the Security Council.

Only the interests of nations could be decided. The court had no jurisdiction over individuals, NGOs, or private enterprises. It was no doubt a good thing that the court was as ineffective as it was. Given muscle, it would only use it against the United States, to take away American freedoms.

U.S. Participation

The United States does participate in the court. Although Clinton signed the treaty in 2000, George W. Bush, a few years later, clarified the U.S. position that the United States had reserved the right to ignore the court's decisions.

To be fair, Clinton hadn't exactly cannonballed into the middle of the international judicial pool. He stuck a toe in. This way, Clinton figured, even though we didn't feel bound to any decisions the court made, we'd make sure that one American judge was on the court at all times.

Both Clinton and Bush expressed their number one concern regarding the UN's court as the prosecution for war crimes of the U.S. military or military personnel. Bush wanted to make it clear that if anyone chose to use the court to hurt the United States, the United States was not going to "be part of the process."

The United States must never submit to this court, Bush said, for it certainly would be used to claim jurisdiction over U.S. military personnel overseas.

Bush's statement brought criticism. Two dozen human rights watchdog groups such as the Rainbow Push Coalition and Amnesty International got together and released a statement. The United States was so concerned about being the subject of the UN's global law-and-order system, those organizations said, that it was giving up an opportunity actively to hunt down and prosecute the human rights violators and war criminals who worked against us.

The point is, the UN has global governing on its mind at all times. It wants to be an organization with teeth, strong enough to bite any nation or interest anywhere in the world—strong enough to rule the world.

Battles Lost

It seems the UN is digging in on every front, entrenching itself in the most anti-American position, sucking at our funds, and degrading our will while boosting our enemies at every turn. Let's take a look at a few of those losing battles in the Middle East and in Africa.

During the early months of 2004, the war in Iraq still dominated the news. America was abuzz with the conflict. Those in favor of the war shouted loud. Those against the war whispered—and then something bad happened to them. They were ridiculed or, in at least one case, someone's cover was blown.

In 2004 George W. Bush and his public relations people were hard at work. The burning questions were:

(1) Can the jihad in Iraq ever end? (2) Could there ever be peace in that nation long enough to sustain a democracy?

One might have assumed that the UN would be concerned with these questions as well, that they would be eager to stop the roadside bombings in Iraq, and that they would help that nation learn to govern itself through democracy.

Not so fast.

How could a democracy work when one candidate threatened the Western world as part of his election campaign? You like a hawk candidate? This was your guy.

Support Sistani or Else

Followers of Iraq's top Shi'ite cleric, Ayatollah Ali al-Sistani, made it clear that it would be a "grave mistake" for the United States and the UN to position themselves in any way in opposition to Sistani and his followers. It was support Sistani or else.

According to Peter Rockas of Reuters, an attempt to delay the Iraqi election by the UN could "stir revolt against their U.S. occupiers." The UN sent a team to Iraq to try to bridge the gap between Washington and the Iraqi Shi'ites.

That bridge was going to have to cover quite a span. Washington wasn't pushing for an election at all but was willing to dish out power gradually to a government of its own choosing.

The majority of Shi'ites, 60 percent of the Iraqi population, who didn't figure to be properly represented by an American-chosen government, said no and pushed for a democratic election—one they were certain to win.

The UN tried to compromise, stating that there would be an election, but it would be delayed, which brought about the threat from Sistani's followers. A message out of Sistani's hometown of Najaf said, "If the UN and Americans do not fulfill the wish of our religious scholars, then *fatwas* will follow. At first there will be demonstrations of civil disobedience and finally armed struggle. We are all behind Sistani, and Shi'ites all have arms. The ball is in the UN's court. If they do not achieve our goals, we will open a front against them. What is this talk that conditions are not ready for elections? . . . Are the only conditions ready the ones that allow Americans to move about and do what they want freely in Iraq?"

Sistani Requests Speedy Elections: Majority Rules

The reclusive Sistani himself, through aides, made it known that he demanded speedy elections. That caused tens of thousands of Iraqis to take to the streets in what was almost exclusively a peaceful demonstration of support.

One powerful Sistani supporter, Sheikh Ali Sweidi, said that the Americans were cunning with their attempts to delay or sidestep general elections in Iraq because "the Shi'ites represent the majority and they have a strong attachment to their religious leaders, so any fatwa to fight America will be followed by all Shi'ites. America and the UN will lose greatly if they oppose the Shi'ite religious authorities."

The Shi'ites were eager to push their weight around. It had been a long time since they'd felt so strong. Saddam kept them weak. Saddam, who represented the minority Sunnis and oppressed the Shi'ites at every opportunity, could not be pushed around. Now that the United States had taken out Saddam, the Shi'ites sensed a huge power vacuum that was going to need filling.

The chain of events put the Shi'ites on a shifting platform when it came to their support of U.S. public policy, for they were certainly in favor of the removal of Saddam and his Sunni regime, but they were just as wholeheartedly against U.S. occupation of Iraq.

When the elections were finally held in 2005, the Sunnis were so convinced that things were fixed that they boycotted the polls. Of the 275 members of the new Iraqi National Assembly to be elected, 180 were Shi'ites and 5 were Sunnis. There were also seventy-five Kurds and fifteen others.

Bush Pushes War in All the Wrong Places

During his presidency, George W. Bush repeatedly called for the UN's cooperation with his global effort to wipe out terrorism. *Washington Times* columnist Arnold Beichman had trouble with Bush's pleas to the UN. He couldn't help but wonder why the pleas. What did Bush hope to accomplish with these statements? Was it just a backhanded insult to the UN because Bush knew no cooperation would be forthcoming? Was it an attempt to make the rest of the world look bad for not stepping up?

Beichman added, "Nor can I understand why Secretary of State Colin Powell had called the UN a 'coalition partner' when it is at best a sneering onlooker."

It made Beichman recall December 9, 1994, the day a UN ten-year resolution passed without opposition. The resolution was called Measures to Eliminate International Terrorism.

The preamble went like this: "Having considered in depth the question of measures to eliminate international terrorism, and convinced that the adoption of the Declaration on Measures to Eliminate International Terrorism should contribute to the struggle against international terrorism...." It demanded that all member states "take all appropriate measures at the national and international levels to eliminate terrorism.... We are deeply disturbed by the worldwide persistence of acts of international terrorism in all its forms and manifestations which endanger or take innocent lives. We are firmly determined to eliminate international terrorism and that those responsible for acts of international terrorism must be brought to justice."

Hollow Words

Looking back, the resolution felt like the setup for a sad joke. As far as Beichman was concerned, this 1994 resolution was the best proof there was that the UN was a fraud. There was a time when the UN believed those words, that there was never justification for terrorism, but the words had grown hollow. He laughed bitterly when he wondered what would happen if such a resolution were introduced at the UN in the twenty-first century.

Then it was Beichman's turn to dream a little. He wrote that in a just world, the UN Security Council would become serious battlers of terrorism, that they would make decisions based on the principles of the 1994 resolution. This, he daydreamed, would cause the UN to form a military force, a coalition, to back up U.S. troops in Iraq, just as the UN had in

1950 when we pulled South Korea's collective ass out of the fire. He didn't say that the chances of his dream coming true were nil. He didn't have to.

Sudan Resolution, Summer of 2004

There were members of the UN who wouldn't criticize Muslims, ever, ever, ever. There could be genocide going on, and they would and they wouldn't disapprove—not if it was in the name of Allah. How do we know? Sudan 2004, that's how.

Sudan is the location of one of the world's oldest civilizations, dating its history back to 3000 B.C., but to call the current situation civilized is a stretch. The country had been placed under an Islamic Legal Code, was divided by civil war, and genocide was going on in the Darfur section, executed by an Islamic group called the Janjawid.

In September 2004, a UN Security Council meeting passed a resolution strongly disapproving of the purge of non-Muslims in Sudan. The resolution said the UN might actually do something if the human rights offenses in Darfur didn't stop. Abdallah Baali—ambassador of Algeria, representing the Arab League—voted nay. The same man had voted against other resolutions on Sudan and had proven himself against any resolution that included the feasibility of intervention. Baali also rejected a resolution calling for Syria to withdraw from Lebanon.

UN as Jihadist Force

Again and again we've seen UN money potentially fund terrorism. In this case, the UN became an ally in the field to terrorists. By fall of 2004 the UN itself had become a *jihadist force*. The evidence concerned the UN Relief and Works Agency (UNRWA), which was allegedly "helping Palestinians attack Israel."

Israel's UN ambassador Dan Gillerman sent a letter to Secretary-

General Kofi Annan demanding he fire the UNRWA commissioner-general Peter Hansen.

Gillerman wrote that the UNRWA was the organization that administered the Palestinian refugee camps and lobbied for the rights of Palestinian refugees to return to their homes safely, the ones that were abandoned in 1948 when the UN carved up Palestine and created the nation of Israel.

The reality of the agency's on-the-ground mission wasn't limited to helping Palestinian refugees, Gillerman points out. He also had documentation that UN ambulances in the Gaza Strip were being used to smuggle weapons for Hamas.

For more than a year, Hamas had a grip on the UNRWA. When Hamas agents ran for leadership roles in the UNRWA workers' union in the Arab refugee camps, they captured 90 percent of the vote and took over. Hamas agents worked for a UN agency, and the American taxpayer paid them in part. Almost a third of the UNRWA's budget came from the United States—more than half from Europe.

Failed Attempt to Criticize Suicide Bombers

On July 7, 2005, suicide bombers executed a series of coordinated attacks on the public transport system of London, England. The bombings were carried out by four British Muslim men who were protesting Great Britain's participation in the Iraq War. Three of the men were of Pakistani descent and one was Jamaican. At 8:50 A.M. three bombs exploded in London almost simultaneously. It was estimated that the explosions took place no more than fifty seconds apart. All three bombs exploded in crowded London Underground trains. Almost an hour later, at 9:47 A.M., a fourth bomb exploded on a double-decker bus in Tavistock Square. The bombs were homemade but effective. They were peroxide based and packed into rucksacks. Fifty-six people were killed in the explosions and more than seven hundred were injured.

Since all four bombers were instantly reduced to smithereens in the attack, we only know who they were and why they did it because two of them videotaped themselves beforehand explaining their motives. They called themselves "soldiers."

As one of the bombers put it, "I and thousands like me are forsaking everything for what we believe. Our drive and motivation doesn't come from tangible commodities that this world has to offer. Our religion is Islam, obedience to the one true God and following the footsteps of the final prophet messenger. Your democratically elected governments continuously perpetuate atrocities against my people all over the world. And your support of them makes you directly responsible, just as I am directly responsible for protecting and avenging my Muslim brothers and sisters. Until we feel security, you will be our targets and until you stop the bombing, gassing, imprisonment, and torture of my people, we will not stop this fight. We are at war and I am a soldier. Now you too will taste the reality of this situation."

The video was broadcast by the Arab television network, Al Jazeera.

Simplest of Moral Discussions

One would think that the simplest of moral discussions—that suicide bombers are bad, for example—would go off without a hitch among the representatives of the UN, this "peacekeeping organization." But even that no-brainer of a condemnation breeds stringent squawks of religious bigotry from Islamic representatives.

During the summer of 2005, the International Humanist and Ethical Union (IHEU), which is as it sounds a world union of humanist organizations, attempted to get a UN subcommittee to condemn killing in the name of religion. The meeting was in Geneva, Switzerland, at a meeting of the UN Subcommittee on Human Rights.

The IHEU thought the condemnation necessary after Islamic clerics, instead of criticizing terrorist attacks on behalf of Allah, made verbal attempts to legitimize the then current wave of attacks. Most notable among these attacks were the July 7, 2005, London attacks.

Shout Down

The IHEU representative requesting the condemnation was David G. Littman, who attempted to address IHEU by reading from a prepared text. The speech was a collaboration of three NGOs: the Association for World Education, the Association of World Citizens, and the IHEU.

Littman's speech never even got started. Each time he began to speak, he was rudely shouted down. The speech was never given, killed by the rude intervention of the subcommission's Islamic members, who shouted that the planned speech was an "attack on Islam."

In reality, as we'll learn in greater detail, the speech was no such thing, but was rather a criticism of prominent Islamic figures who had encouraged extremism. The speech, to put it simply, called for a condemnation of "calls to kill" in the name of God or *any* religion.

The point was an important one.

High-ranking Muslim clerics said suicide bombers remained Muslims, and that British civilians were a legitimate target for jihad. Among the proponents of the "terrorism is good" school was Qatar University dean of Islamic law.

When the president of the IHEU, Roy Brown, found out that the planned speech had been prevented by the Islamic members of the Human Rights subcommittee, he said, "This is part and parcel of the refusal by the Islamic representatives at the UN to condemn the suicide bombers or to accept any criticism of those who kill innocent people in the name of God."

Brown noted that this was not the first time the Islamic members of the same subcommittee had framed topics regarding terrorism as attempts to defame Islam. A similar incident occurred during the spring of 2005.

"It is high time," Brown continued, "that the Islamic states at the UN recognized that the suicide bombers are acting in the name of their religion, and to unequivocally condemn their actions."

Littman: "Terrorism in the Name of God"

Although Littman's speech was never read, copies were circulated and the text was published on the Internet. In the opening line, Littman set the tone, saying that he felt it appropriate to address what had previously been considered a taboo subject at the UN, the "radical ideology of jihad that includes calls for killing and terrorism in the name of God."

That was the point at which the shouting began. If allowed, Littman would have discussed a July 18, 2005, fatwa issued by the British Muslim Forum and approved by five hundred Islamic clerics across the United Kingdom stating that those who believed in killing innocent people in the name of God were not real Muslims. A major conference of 170 Muslim scholars rebutted by saying that terrorists were real Muslims. The rebuttal said the only way to become an apostate was to fail to believe in Allah. Therefore killing innocent people in the name of Allah was indeed a "real Muslim" thing to do.

Victims of Jihad

A great deal of research went into Littman's intended speech. Much of the subject matter came out of an April 18, 2005, conference entitled "Victims of Jihad: Muslims, Dhimmis, Apostates, and Women."

The conference was attended by historians, writers, and human rights defenders. A background historical analysis of jihad was presented by Utrecht University academic Johannes Jansen of the Netherlands. Dutch parliamentarian Ayaan Hirsi Ali discussed the mistreatment of women in the Islamic world. A warning was given by Dr. Ahmad Abu Matar, a Palestinian academic living in Oslo, who said many European Muslims felt anxiety over coexisting with those practicing an extremist fundamentalist version of Islam, but were too frightened of those elements to speak out about their troubled feelings.

"Mr. Chairman, the most essential and basic human right is the right to live!" Littman's speech read (exclamation point included). He quoted from a 1981 UN General Assembly document titled "Holy Jihad" that explained "to the world that Holy Jihad is an Islamic concept which may not be misinterpreted or misconstrued, and that the practical measures to put it into effect would be in accordance with that concept and by incessant consultations among Islamic states." In 1982 Hezbollah commenced jihadist bombings and hostage taking in southern Lebanon. Hamas soon joined the ranks.

The speech made reference to the 1988 Hamas charter, coauthored by the late Sheikh Ahmad Yassin and Abd al-Aziz al-Rantissi, which openly called for genocide. The charter paraphrased the Muslim Brotherhood's Charter of 1928, which declared that, "Allah is its target, the Prophet is its model, the Koran its Constitution; Jihad is its path, and death for the sake of Allah is the loftiest of its wishes."

"Cult of Hatred and Death"

On December 30, 2002, Hamas leader al-Rantissi reacted to America's buildup for war in Iraq by calling for that nation to be flooded with "Islamikazes" (short for Islamic kamikazes). Al-Rantissi said, "The enemies of Allah . . . crave life while the Muslims crave martyrdom. The martyrdom operations that shock can ensure that horror is sowed in the enemies' hearts, and horror is one of the causes of defeat."

To that the IHEU called for an "unambiguous rejection of this murderous cult of hatred and death." Only with the absolute condemnation could the "grave dangers of a clash of cultures and civilizations be avoided."

Although a smattering of objections from moderate Muslims followed each terrorist attack, they were mild and passive. There was, as Richard Nixon might have put it, a "silent majority" that offered Islamic extremism silent approval.

Littman made it clear in his speech that he agreed wholeheartedly with both of these statements by quoting the English seventeenth-century poet John Donne, who wrote that we are all "involved in mankind."

Summing up, Littman was to have said, "The time has come for distinguished representatives of the Organization of the Islamic Conference (OIC), the Arab League, and individual Muslim religious and secular leaders to be heard at the United Nations, united in an unambiguous condemnation of those who defame Islam by calls to kill in the name of Allah." He then would have called on the subcommittee to adopt a resolution to condemn categorically any "call to kill, to terrorize, or to use violence in the name of God or of any religion."

Absurdity of Muslims Condemning Muslims

Not long after the July 7 attacks, Amir Taheri, a communist writing for a London Arab daily, took a major step in the right direction by writing: "Until we hear the voices of Muslims condemning attacks with no words of qualification such as 'but' and 'if,' the suicide bombers and the murderers will have an excuse to think they enjoy the support of all Muslims. The real battle against the enemy of mankind will begin when the 'silent majority' in the Islamic world makes its voice heard against the murderers, and against those who brainwash them, and fund them."

Around the same time TV director Abd al-Rahman al-Rashed wrote an article titled "Expel Extremism Today" in which he said, "For over ten years now, I myself and other Arab writers have warned against the dangers of the reckless handling of the extremism that is now spreading like a plague within the British community."

He called extremism a contagious disease and slammed Great Britain for going easy on the Arab and Muslim intellectuals who wrote proextremism editorials and sang the praises of war criminals such as bin-Laden and al-Zarqawi.

Al-Rashed said he didn't believe that all those editorial writers were genuinely supportive of extremist behavior, but that they were rather too frightened of those same extremists to take an opposing view.

Loosening the UN's Grip on Civilization

The board vice president of *Jihad Watch*, Hugh Fitzgerald, believed Islamic extremism was to the UN as Hitler was to the League of Nations. As soon as enemies of freedom were allowed to join the UN, the place went downhill fast. Writing soon after the 7/7 attacks (London bombings), Fitzgerald said that allowing the bad guys in was the moment the civilized organization first loosened its grip on civilization. The disease grew. The UN's Arab bloc was at the core of a larger Islamic bloc. That in turn called the shots among less-powerful African nations that bought into a bogus sense of Third World unity.

How ironic that the African poor fell in line with the Arabs who could barely stand because of the amount of bling they wore to meetings.

Deafening Silence

A deafening silence, a tintinnabulation of mind-numbing nothingness, came from the Muslim delegates when it came to the despicable terrorist acts being committed. Since 1967 there had been no criticism from the Islamic bloc for any Islamic extremist attack on a non-Muslim target. Even if that target included schoolgirls or the elderly. Even if the incident terrorized the world by taking place during the Winter Olympics. Even if Egyptian bombers took out Christian civilians in Biafra, or even if the 200,000 dead were from a genocide as Indonesia took over Christian East Timor.

The UN was both corrupt and corrupting, yet its machinations—its theatrics!—were still taken seriously by U.S. and international media. This, Fitzgerald opined, was ridiculous.

The UN was an organization that would never have the teeth to stop the genocidal jihad in Darfur and Israel or the proliferation of nuclear weapons into rogue nations such as Iran. There would be no time at the UN for any of that, too busy it would be on other matters, like allocating relief money for the "Palestinian people."

Familiar Dilemma

Genocide was a dilemma that would have struck the delegates of the League of Nations as extremely familiar back in the day of Hitler in the Rhineland, fascists in Spain, and Japanese in China. The UN was an organization that had been undermined from within, undermined by a belief system that left its adherents "intellectually impoverished."

Phrases that rang with hope when the UN was born out of World War II's ashes, phrases like "international community," were now just sick humor. The biggest laugh came from the name of the organization itself, United Nations. United? Hardly.

Free Speech R.I.P.

As we saw with the squelching of Littman's UN speech calling for moderate Muslims to condemn terrorism in the name of God, freedom of speech is not held as sacred by many UN members. Here are some other examples of how the First Amendment, a freedom we take for granted, isn't held so dear inside the UN's tower of secrets.

Speak No Evil

During the summer of 2008, a rule was changed regarding meetings of the UN Human Rights Council. Muslim countries had worked since the inception of the council to prevent Islam from being criticized during debate, and they now had successfully gotten the new rule passed.

To some the rule was a no-brainer. UN meetings should be, like saloon conversations, governed by a no-religion, no-politics rule. Others were more realistic. The rule was impossible when it came to human rights discussions since so much of man's inhumanity to man stemmed from religious and political differences. To ban discussions involving Islam could be interpreted to mean that jihad itself was a taboo subject.

The spokesman for the new rule was Council president Doru-Romulus Costea who explained that once UN debates swerved into religion they had a tendency not to swerve back out again. Religion caused the debate to become "very complex, very sensitive, and very intense." Costea added that the council was not made up of theologians, and the members were not prepared to undertake an in-depth discussion of religion. "Consequently we should not do it," he said. While the rhetoric clung to religions in general, everyone knew the topic was one religion in particular. Representatives from Muslim nations who didn't care for the way Islam was being discussed brought about this ban.

Stoning and Genital Mutilation

As an example of the way in which the new rule would poorly affect the conversation regarding human rights, Western nations would no longer be able to use the Human Rights Council to denounce female genital mutilation as well as the practice of stoning, standard punishment for adultery in Muslim nations. Since both practices were considered sanctioned by Islamic Law, their subject could no longer be broached by the council.

Not long after the new rule was adopted, a representative of the Association for World Education, an NGO, sought to deliver a joint statement with the HEU to protest genital mutilation. Not so fast. Representatives from Egypt, Pakistan, and Iran angrily interrupted the speaker, saying it was against the rules for the council to hear arguments against the Law of Islam. The Pakistani representative, Imran Ahmed Siddiqui, said that the denouncing of certain practices in the Muslim world was an "out-of-context discussion of the law." He asked that the speech be stopped.

A representative from Slovenia took up the cause of free speech and reminded the Pakistani representative that all nongovernment representatives had the right to "make a statement within the merits of the agenda item under discussion." Slovenia saw no grounds for any "restricting censorship" in this case.

The Egyptian delegate sharply disagreed. The topic was of "religious sensitivity" and therefore forbidden.

Eventually, the representative of the Association for World Education, Littman, did get to speak and managed to get on the record that a particularly brutal form of female genital mutilation known as infibulation had been performed on "almost 90 percent of the female population in one region in the north of Sudan."

Littman concluded, "We believe that only a fatwa from al-Azhar Grand Sheikh Sayed Tantawi—replacing the fatwas of 1949, 1951, and 1981—will change this barbaric criminal practice, which is now growing even in Europe."

Egypt again interrupted, "This is an attempt to raise a bad traditional practice to Islam. Sheikh al-Azhar is the president of the largest and the biggest and the oldest Islamic university in the world. My point is that Islam will not be crucified in the council."

Germany got into the act, asking for a confirmation of the interpretation he'd just heard and, once confirmed, objecting strongly to the use by the Egyptian of the word "crucifixion," which flew in the face of the new rule prohibiting reference to religion and its symbols during discussions.

Egypt ignored this suggestion and demanded that Littman's statement about the fatwas be stricken from the record. Littman defended his statement, noting that Sheikh al-Azhar was on the record stating that all men and women needed to be circumcised and circumcision "does honor" to women.

Littman continued speaking, noting that in Iran, Sudan, and other countries women are still routinely stoned to death for adultery. In Iran, he noted, the women were buried up to their waists and were pummeled only with blunt stones, so as to prolong their agony before death.

This statement brought a protest from the Iranian delegate who said the statement was false and had nothing to do with reality in his country. Littman countered with a statement that as of 2007 there were eight women on Iran's version of death row, awaiting death by stoning.

Littman's statements were true, but that meant nothing to the delegates from Iran, Pakistan, and Egypt who were concerned only because they saw them as an insult to Islam.

It was noted that the same loud Islamic voices who indirectly supported the stoning and circumcision of woman also called for the *prosecution* of Dutch politician and filmmaker Geert Wilders and Danish cartoonist Kurt Westergaard for his drawing of Muhammad with a bomb in his turban as well as any freely speaking human who made comments that they perceived to be insulting to Islam.

Freedom of speech of course survives, but the forces of extremism are chipping away at it little by little—especially at the UN's Human Rights Council.

The Great Money Suck

During the autumn of 2008, Jerusalem journalist Arlene Kushner filed a report for *Front Page Magazine* pointing out the ways in which the UN applied selective thinking when planning its funding of Middle East programs.

Only weeks before Kushner's report, the UN announced a "2009 Consolidated Appeal," an attempt to raise close to a half a billion dollars for UN and NGO humanitarian-assistance programs. The presentation in Jerusalem included statements by Maxwell Gaylard, the UN's Humanitarian Coordinator; Philippe Lazzarini, the head of the UN Office for the Coordination of Humanitarian Affairs; and Filippo Grandi, the deputy commissioner-general of the UN Relief and Works Agency (UNRWA).

That money, it was announced, would go to aid those living in "occupied Palestinian Territories" and for the UNRWA, which gave shelter and food to Palestinian Arab refugees.

Ideological Blind Spot

The distribution of the money could not have been more one-sided. As was typical, the UN took a wholly anti-Israel, anti-U.S. view of matters. The UN was quick to condemn Israeli military actions, but very slow to criticize Palestinian terrorism. Kushner called this one-sided worldview an ideological blind spot.

The announcement of the fund-raising effort by Gaylard, Lazzarini, and Grandi harped on Israeli misconduct. It was agreed that Palestinians had it rough. The Israeli closure of Gaza was of utmost concern, they said. The Israelis said Gaza should remain closed as long as Palestinian rockets continue to fall in Israel, but in the meantime, even basic supplies were prevented from crossing into Gaza to reach the Palestinian people.

Lazzarini said that, from the UN's viewpoint, Gaza represented a "humanitarian crisis." The closure of Gaza, he said, deprived the Palestinians there of every human right.

Even though a truce between Israel and Hamas had been in place for several months, the amount of supplies moving from Israel into Gaza only increased by 20 percent. Israel, Lazzarini complained, was still not allowing UNRWA supply trucks into Gaza on a daily basis. Often the supplies were turned away at the border by Israeli soldiers.

UNtrustworthy

Despite the two-way nature of the conflict along the Israeli-Gaza border, no UN officials were wasting any tears on Israel. Israel's understandable stance was that until the UN sufficiently condemned the launching of rockets from Gaza into Israel, they were not to be trusted as arbiters of the conflict. Where was the UN when, on November 29, 2008, the same day that supply trucks were not allowed into Gaza, a Palestinian rocket landed inside Israel?

Lack of trust for the UN in the region aggravated the situation. The UN was not impartial, so why should Israeli soldiers allow UN supply trucks to cross into Palestine? Supply trucks from other organizations were allowed through, and the Israelis even repaired the Kerem Shalom crossing so that moving supplies into Gaza would be easier.

Another factor the UN failed to mention in its presentation was that the Israeli guards in charge of stopping or letting supply trucks through at the checkpoints were themselves under the threat of attack from inside Gaza.

"Israelis risk their lives so that goods can move through," Kushner wrote. UN tunnel vision was absolute. How many times had the UN condemned, or even mentioned, the attacks on checkpoints from inside Gaza, slowing the flow of supplies? Zero. The UN's relentless focus on Israel's hesitance to open up the Gaza border distracted attention away from the many tunnels under the Israel-Gaza border that serve to smuggle weapons to Hamas.

Rescuing Hamas

By January 2009 the UN's position in the region became even more blatantly anti-Israel. The organization, in fact, appeared determined to rescue Hamas terrorists even as they were on the verge of military defeat at the hands of the Israeli military and even despite the clear-cut fact that Hamas had started the current military crisis by firing hundreds of rockets into Israel, targeting civilians and terrorizing women and children.

It was Hamas that had refused a ceasefire extension, a ceasefire they had been ignoring anyway. Israel had responded militarily only when provoked. Using military force in self-defense was permissible according to section 51 of the UN Charter.

But what did the UN do? On January 8, 2009, they adopted a resolution calling for an immediate ceasefire in the region and the immediate and full withdrawal of Israeli troops from Gaza. The resolution said nothing about Hamas being a terrorist state, or about halting the launching of rockets into Israel from Gaza, or about Hamas agents using women and children as human shields as they went about their terrorist activities. You find a Hamas rocket-firing location inside Gaza, and you were bound to find a school or a hospital nearby.

A careful read revealed that the word "Hamas" did not appear anywhere in the resolution. The resolution was worded to gel with the Islamic version of history, that the Israelis were the real terrorists and that Hamas and other organizations of their ilk were "resistance fighters," battling bravely against their persecutors.

The resolution did mention the UNRWA and its efforts to bring relief to Gaza. According to some reports, this effort wasn't just working on the wrong side, it was openly working against the enemy Israeli army.

Much of the delivered supplies went to refugee camps in Gaza that were merely a cover for bases of terrorist operations, such as small-arms factories, explosives laboratories, and arms caches. The UN vehicles themselves, reports said, were used to transport Hamas terrorists, arms, and explosives. Terrorist organizations, reports said, were discovered to be working out of UNRWA offices.

Laying Blame

In November of 2007, according to the UN News Centre, Palestinian militants entered a school in the Gaza strip run by a UN agency helping Palestinian refugees. From the otherwise empty school, the terrorists launched rockets aimed at Israel. When Israel responded by firing on the rocket-launcher's location, Navanethem Pillay, the UN High Commissioner for Human Rights, and other UN officials were eager to blame civilian casualties on Israel.

Hamas, ever opportunistic for a public relations coup, made sure the media got plenty of photos of the civilian casualties so the damage done by the "Israeli bullies" could be seen by the world. Pillay made her comments during the ninth special session of the UN's Human Rights Council, and like the first eight, the ninth was dedicated to condemning Israel.

To be fair, Pillay did tag onto her statement an addendum stating that any action on the part of "Israel's opponent" to put civilians in harm's way was "strictly prohibited under international law." Still, the statement was slanted against Israel, just like everything else that came out of the UN.

Nowhere was it mentioned that Hamas not Israel was the force that violated the Geneva Convention when it targeted civilians, impersonated civilians or police in order to dish out terror, and hid behind human shields.

Seeking Lasting Peace

Ignored was the fact that it had historically been Israel and not the Palestinians who sought out a lasting peace. The only caveat the Israelis demanded was that they would not agree to anything that would make their people less secure or further put civilians in harm's way.

Hamas had never made any effort toward a lasting peace. It had repeatedly viewed negotiated ceasefires as an excuse to build up its military capability. Not long before his death in an Israeli bombing attack, Hamas leader Nizar Rayyan said that he could envision a fifty-year ceasefire only as an opportunity to strengthen Hamas militarily and to prepare it for, after the fifty years had passed, the final battle.

"Israel is an impossibility," Rayyan said. "It is an offense against God."

The UN further ignored the historical fact that Israel had once before unilaterally withdrawn from Gaza in 2005.

America's Jelly Spine

The UN resolution worked under the premise that Israel controlled Gaza and was therefore responsible for the welfare of the population there, a population that was in actuality under Hamas control. The resolution condemned all violence in the region, especially that directed against civilians, but failed to mention which side participated in these forbidden activities. The resolution condemned terrorism in the region but ignored the fact that Hamas unleashed the terror.

The United States had a vote in this resolution and, with a spine of jelly, abstained. The United States could have used its veto power to kill the anti-Israeli resolution but chose not to. The only action singled out by the resolution was the military occupation of Gaza by Israel. This wording allowed the spin doctors who hated Israel to go hog wild.

Toughening Up?

During the first half of 2009, plans were made to do something about the corruption within the UN Human Rights Council. A bill was written that would withhold U.S. funds from the UN until such a time as it saw the light and began to treat the United States and its allies fairly.

During May, the UN General Assembly voted on how to fill the eighteen seats on the Human Rights Council. The United States ran for a three-year term on the council and was elected. That put the leader of all free nations sitting side by side with several countries that had questionable human rights histories. These included Cuba, China, Saudi Arabia, and Russia.

Obama reportedly believed the council could be "reformed from within," but most believed that wasn't what would happen. The United States would simply lose every vote.

The Stearns Bill

The plan to withhold funds was the brainchild of Congressman Cliff Stearns of Florida. His bill called for the outing of the Human Rights Council as a "table for tyrants" and pledged to withhold funds until the council "mended its ways." The bill condemned the council as being no improvement over its predecessor, the UN Commission on Human Rights.

The bill said, "The UN Human Rights Council does not embody the recommended institutional reforms necessary to advance human rights." Its voting system was defective because it relied on "geographic quotas that will only ensure that human rights abusers will continue to have access to membership on the council." The geographic quota system, it said, ensured a majority of membership slots for the world's least democratic regions.

The bill pointed out that with Asia and Africa making up a majority of the council, it was biased against Western democracies, which received only 15 percent of the vote. Israel was not allowed to join the council, which routinely passed resolutions that condemned Israel and portrayed Israel as the demon in the Middle East.

Stearns' bill said the council must meet three criteria for the United States to continue its support: (1) The council must be a body that upheld the ideals enumerated in the UN Charter and the Universal Declaration of Human Rights, (2) the council should allow full participation by Israel, and (3) the council should be composed of countries that hold regular competitive democratic elections and have a "credible civil society."

Previous bills along these same lines had been introduced to the House of Representatives before but never got very far and expired before any legitimate debate could take place. During the second Bush administration, the United States silently protested the council by refusing to join it, but that strategy flew out the window with the Obama regime.

The Stearns bill might eventually go the same route, and early predictions were that it would be "buried in committee."

Sticking Israel with the Bill

During the early summer of 2009, correspondent Anav Silverman filed a troubling message about the UN for the Sderot Media Center in Sderot, Israel. The dispatch began by referencing the May 2009 184-page UN report that condemned Israel for damage done to UN equipment during the war along the Gaza Strip. The report accused Israel of "negligence or recklessness." The UN secretary-general Ban Ki-moon rejected a call for an impartial and full review of the war and said the UN was seeking $11 million from Israel as compensation for the stuff they blew up.

Responsible for this report was Ian Martin, former head of Amnesty International, who complained specifically of nine incidents in which Israeli military actions damaged UN equipment.

There were ten incidents in all described in the UN report. Only one protested Palestinian actions (a Palestinian rocket hit a UN warehouse, $30,000 damage). Silverman read all 184 pages and said there wasn't one mention in the UN report of the fortune in damages Hamas had caused, raining their terrorist rockets onto schools in south Israel.

Typical.

The UN's Development Program

The suspiciously one-sided nature of the UN's funding process became apparent at the other end of the Middle East during the summer of 2008. What looked like a humanitarian program turned out to be a sophisticated money-laundering operation for an evil regime.

The problem was reportedly with the UN Development Program (UNDP), a powerful subdivision that controlled a full quarter of the UN's $20 billion budget. Though UNDP was funded internationally, the United States was humanitarian number one with more than $100 million annual contributions. Among the UNDP's responsibilities was to determine the funding necessary for external programs.

With all that power over the UN's finances, you'd think that the UNDP would be particularly clean, squeaky clean. But no. The program was just as scandal ridden as other UN misadventures.

UN Bank

While the UNDP's name indicated involvement in hands-on developing in parts of the world where development was most desperately needed, the program did not view itself that way—at least not exclusively. The UNDP thought of itself as a bank—a bank that wrote checks, with zero public relations duty. American taxpayers never knew how much money the program sent or where because the UNDP was under no obligation to divulge its activities, so it didn't.

Even in corrupt-to-the-core countries, the UNDP would send a check and instruct that nation to implement the development program on its own. Now even the smallest schoolchild could see where that was headed.

The dictator was going to spend the money on development all right, on the development of a new bunker residence for himself.

There was no way to know for sure where the money went. A whistle-blower from within the UNDP's money-transferring system admitted that the money's final destination was beyond the program's scope. For example, the whistle-blower revealed, the money sent to North Korea could be traced only until its arrival in Pyongyang, at which point it disappeared.

Left Hand Slaps Right

Not only did the UNDP throw billions of dollars into the wind, but they did it right out in the open—so open that they were caught by the UN's own investigation. We don't know everything, but assembling the intelligence, we do know a picture starts to form. We can make some strong educated guesses. The UNDP had a relationship with North Korea: the program gave the North Korean government money.

The investigation revealed that the UNDP didn't seem to care what was done with the money they sent to various countries. Sometimes the recipient was the government; sometimes it was NGO cutouts for the government.

In either case, no attempt was made to trace the money to a provable development project. No attempt was made to verify that the organizations the UN contributed to were legitimate. For all the program knew, it could have been sending its money to an individual or a corporation—sending development greenbacks where there wasn't any development.

For observers, a question burned, "What does the UNDP get in return?"

Corrupt... *and* Dangerous

It was bad enough that the UNDP's money was not reaching its intended target. Worse, it did nothing to prevent the money from funding terrorist groups. Checks were written so carelessly that a recipient would only need the flimsiest of covers to make the UN money list. If they sent money to North Korea, can there be a place where they wouldn't send money?

When you read any UNDP comment about North Korea, you'd swear its rhetoric was straight out of a little leather-bound book of whiney communist propaganda. North Korea sounded like a beaten wife, its ego propped up with antidepressants: "North Korea is so great, but small and meek—the United States, so big and mean."

How would Mr. and Mrs. America feel if they knew the check they sent to the IRS was, in part, going to install an indoor-outdoor swimming pool for an opium magnate or buy a new whip for the trafficker of stolen women?

What's a Crusade Without Persia?

Among the places the UNDP was pumping cash was Iran. If this wasn't a money-laundering operation, it certainly resembled one. The UNDP promised to send $177 million to Iran spread out from 2005 to 2009. That money was to be paid by the program's cutout, the United Nations Development Assistance Framework (UNDAF).

This contribution to a primary sponsor to terrorism was shocking enough on the surface. Looking closer, it got worse. The money went to the Iranian Ministry of Foreign Affairs, the head of which once addressed the UN, saying Iran was never going to stop its nuclear enrichment program no matter how many sanctions were placed on them.

Asked about the money going from the UN to Iran, the UNDP said the money was going to help Iran "obtain potential dual-use technology." It was a "transfer of knowledge in science and technology through technology-based services." The UN hoped the new technology would help Iran "advance processing technologies and innovative system design."

When an enemy was trying to develop the capability to make and deliver a nuclear weapon, maybe helping them with its knowledge of technology wasn't the best idea. Right?

A Plump Persian Purse

In addition to sending money directly to Iran, the UNDP also helped Iranian causes to receive UN money from another slice of the UN's budget pie. The World Health Organization and UNESCO—in addition to the UNDP—were "partners" with a group called the Iranian Research Organization for Science and Technology (IROST).

Japanese intelligence looked into IROST and discovered these Iranians had, at least in the past, worked in developing chemical and biological weapons and had expressed an interest in nuclear proliferation.

British intelligence investigated the Iranian organization as well and learned that it had procured goods and technology for weapons-of-mass-destruction programs. Among the frightening items the Iranian organization sought were weaponized fungus and toxins, British intelligence reported.

Even if you assumed that the money really was for the technology (and not for a rich man's second yacht), it was still so wrong! How could one argue that, of all the places on earth, Iran was the place that most desperately needed this type of funding?

Let's not forget, Iran was not a poor country. They had too much oil and gas to be poor. So more questions were raised than answered by reports from spies within the Iranian organization that the UN money was actually being used to boost Iran's economy and being used as a catalyst for importing, exporting, and producing.

How 'Bout Some for Detroit?

The UN money was also being funneled into Iran's number-one car manufacturer, Iran Khodro. The idea was to help them produce and export more cars, ignoring the fact that they were already the area's richest carmaker. Khodro made 650,000 cars annually anyway and was enjoying a 23 percent annual growth—and, like a malingerer, they accepted relief from the UN.

As all of this was going on, the UN Security Council, in theory the organization's most powerful body, placed economic sanctions on Iran, sanctions that were systematically undermined by the UNDP.

The Wall Street Journal Shadows the Moolah

Give credit to *The Wall Street Journal* for digging out some of these facts. The reporters there were very good at following the money, and they revealed that on the occasions in which the UNDP admitted to sending money to evil regimes on both sides of the world, they still underestimated the amounts.

The UNDP claimed its annual payment to North Korean organizations was $30 million, yet the *Journal* found that the figure had to be close to twice that much. The UNDP apologized for the error and said that its math must have been faulty.

The *Journal* discovered that more than $11 million of the UNDP's annual North Korean budget was going directly to Kim Jong-il. The *Journal* knew where to look because of the courage of then diplomat Mark Wallace who exposed the UNDP's "shenanigans."

The *Journal* pulled up short of saying that the UNDP and North Korea appeared to be in cahoots about something, but they did say that taking the facts at face value the very least the UNDP could be accused of was allowing themselves to be duped by corrupt North Koreans.

Blood Money

Of particular concern was the possibility North Korea was using the money supplied by the UN to increase its military capabilities. The cover story turned out to be that the money was scheduled to be spent on non-state-of-the-art technology that would allow the North Koreans to make better maps and thus be able to manage ecological concerns better. Of course, the actual destination of the money remained anyone's guess.

The UNDP story forced "action" by the U.S. government. There were calls to cut the amount of money drastically that was contributed each year to the UNDP. A *Journal* editorial, a follow-up to their own investigation, noted that the UNDP's executive board had a responsibility to allow better oversight of its programs. This, the paper noted, was particularly true *when the money was going to countries ruled by a dictator*. The paper called for a resolution that would require the UNDP to adhere to American import and export laws and force the program to hire outside auditors to keep track of the flow of UNDP money.

Alliance of (Anti-American) Civilizations

UN leaders have demonstrated a nasty habit of pursuing their anti-American goals even after leaving the UN. Former secretary general Kofi Annan, for example, left the UN but continued to smash away at what was left of American popularity abroad.

Annan became the proponent of a UN-sponsored initiative called the Alliance of Civilizations (AOC). Thomas P. Kilgannon, president of Freedom Alliance, claimed the initiative, which on its surface appeared to be a catalyst for generic international friendliness—Kilgannon called it a "why can't we all just get along" club—was actually a public relations arm, cocked and ready to sling mud in Uncle Sam's eye.

The initiative's stated purpose was "to bridge divides and overcome prejudice, misconceptions, misperceptions, and polarization which potentially threaten world peace."

A vacant-eyed beauty-pageant contestant couldn't have put it better. She wants world peace. But look closer at the initiative, and you find another humongous money suck, vacuuming funds from U.S. coffers and delivering that cash by the truckload to the Third World.

It also advocated an increased power and sense of responsibility in the UN and urged that the organization play umpire in all the world's international disagreements—sole arbiter of a global government.

But how can we accept the utopian visions of any starry-eyed group when that vision paints a world without Israel or a world in which human rights abusers thrive?

Guiding Principles

If you take a peak at the AOC's "Guiding Principles," you find the phrase "terrorism can never be justified." What is terrorism? The UN has never agreed on a definition.

The initiative also spends a lot of time explaining why money, more money, should be taken from the United States and transferred to poorer nations. The reason: "Western powers maintain overwhelming political, economic, and military power in the world."

When the initiative isn't grinding away at U.S. power and prestige, it is glorifying Islam and apologizing for Islamic extremism: "Islam is being perceived by some as an inherently violent religion," the AOC's guidelines complain with a straight face. "But such views are at best manifestly incorrect and at worst maliciously motivated."

Not a Peep from the Peanut Gallery

The fact was that the extremists performed their terrorism without rebuke from nonextremist Muslims. There was the problem. Islamics denouncing terrorism in the name of Allah were as rare as sushi at a NASCAR race.

The initiative ignored this global phenomenon, and instead it claimed that the world's problems, like hatred, had nothing to do with Islamic activism or militancy. Who was to blame? You guessed it; it was Old Glory's fault.

The AOC put it in writing: "The violent manifestations between the United States and Muslim countries are due to the invasion of certain Muslim countries by Western military forces and their continued presence in these countries." Got that? The 9/11 attacks had nothing to do with it.

Hollywood Propaganda and Other Villains

Another villain was Hollywood. The movies "fueled hostile perceptions" by using Muslims as villains but never heroes. There was an urgent "need for balanced images of ordinary Muslims in Western mass media."

In the Western news media, "an appreciably more nationalistic and at times anti-Muslim tone has become evident in news and commentary." And about Al Jazeera and other anti-American media around the world, the AOC remains predictably mum.

The AOC had a plan to improve American colleges and universities: their libraries should be graced with "publications coming from the Muslim world on a range of subjects related to Islam and the Muslim world."

And who's in the AOC? Representatives from Turkey, Iran, Qatar, Egypt, Tunisia, and Morocco as well as other nations. There were only two from the United States and one of them is Professor John Esposito from the Prince al-Waleed bin-Talal Center for Muslim-Christian Understanding at Georgetown University.

And to rub our nose in it, the United States coughed up the great bulk of the AOC's budget. Even environmentalists would have to disapprove of this tree-killing organization, one of the world's largest producers of anti-American propaganda.

The Great Anti-American Vacuum continues to suck.

Bending the News

Though there are reporters who are willing to stick up for Israel and the United States, there is a worldwide anti-American bias when it comes to journalism. This fact is most evident in the Middle East.

News out of the Israel-Gaza border was bent, slanted by the terrorists who could spin stories (or flat-out fabricate stories) that framed the Palestinians in the best possible light. The region's proterrorist media was responsible for the bias.

Jabaliya Incident

Take for example the occasion during the first days of 2009 when the UN reported that Israeli shells had struck a UN school in Jabaliya, Gaza, killing forty-three civilians. The report was specific, and seemed to be fact filled. The report said that the shells were launched by the Israeli Defense Forces on January 6. The building struck was a UN Relief and Works Agency (UNRWA) school.

The story appeared in a wide variety of media, not all of it from the "usual suspects" of proterrorist propaganda. CNN ran the story as well as France24, *China Daily*, and BBC World. The old gray lady, *The New York Times*, also ran the story, but as a tribute to their long-lived journalistic integrity, they added the word "Reportedly" to their headline.

Three weeks later, those global news services kept mum as a Canadian international newspaper said "not so fast" when it came to the report of the January 6 shelling. Its reporter, Patrick Martin, had sought in vain to confirm the report independently. Turned out, the shell had hit the school as advertised, but the whole truth had gone unreported.

An eyewitness to the event said that no one inside the building was killed. All the casualties had been to people standing outside the school on the street at the time of the shelling. The eyewitness refused to identify himself other than as a teacher at the school. Asked why the secrecy, the teacher said he'd been told by representatives of the UNRWA not to discuss the things he'd seen with reporters.

Excuses, Excuses

Once the veracity of the initial report was under question, the UNRWA did its best to cover its own backside by denying that they ever said anyone inside the school had been killed.

The director of UNRWA operations in Gaza, John Ging, said they had not been specific about the location of the casualties and that the inside-the-school detail had been picked up along the curvaceous journalistic road by outlets that subsequently published the report.

This complaint was disingenuous, however, as a review of the transcript shows Ging had been most insistent that Israel was the devil for what they had done with their flying explosives.

According to the *European Observer* on the day following the attack, Ging said that the attack was "horrific." He explained that his organization had supplied the military with the GPS location of every one of their schools, and yet the bomb hit the school nonetheless. Ging made it clear that he felt this was proof that Israel had purposefully bombed a school inside Gaza. "It is very clear that these are UN installations," Ging added.

Must've Been a Typo

Did the UN ever admit that they had been party to misinforming the public about military operations inside Gaza. On February 2, 2009, about a month after the incident, the UN humanitarian coordinator in Jerusalem, Maxwell Gaylord, acknowledged the misrepresentation of the facts and blamed a "typo" for the misunderstanding.

At that time he made it clear that in addition to all the casualties occurring outside the UN school, all the missiles had struck outside the school as well.

Goldstone

In June 2009 the UN further revealed its penchant for shaping public opinion against Israel and against the United States. The UN had formed a UN Fact Finding Mission on the Gaza Conflict, headed by Judge Richard Goldstone of South Africa and sponsored by the UN Human Rights Council. Israel refused to cooperate with this mission, citing a clear anti-Israeli bias test case proven by those undertaking the fact-finding effort.

The UN Human Rights Council conducted several investigations into Israeli mistreatment of Palestinians in Gaza but had never once investigated the impact of those in south Israel who had to endure aerial attacks from terrorist groups inside Gaza.

One member of the team was Christine Chinkin, professor of law at the London School of Economics, who in published works called Israel's antiterrorist activities along the Gaza Strip "war crimes." The phrase was even more common in Gaza, where a Hamas official said he looked forward to the results of the UN fact-finding mission as he expected it to be "like ammunition in the hands of the people who are willing to sue Israeli war criminals."

Goldstone released the results of his fact-finding mission in late 2009.

The report said Israel used excessive force and deliberately targeted civilians in heavily populated areas. It was a laundry list of alleged human rights violations by Israel.

In response, at the end of January 2010, Israel submitted a forty-six-page report to the UN in which it denied everything. Israel argued that their missile attacks were legitimate acts of self-defense, retaliation for Palestinian and Hamas rocket attacks from the Gaza Strip.

Call for an Independent Commission

The UN report had called for an independent commission to investigate military actions along the Israel-Gaza border. Israel rejected this idea. If the cards were marked and the deck was stacked, Israel didn't want to play the UN's game.

Israeli analyst Gerald Steinberg told the Voice of America that Israel had nothing to gain by cooperating with the UN's "kangaroo court." He said the Goldstone report was a fabrication based on false claims. Sure, some of the claims had a basis in reality, but even those were taken out of context and tilted. Steinberg said the best thing the Israeli government could do was to expose the Goldstone report as a farce.

Not all Israeli advocates agreed with Steinberg's position. Israeli analyst Hirsch Goodman said ignoring the Goldstone Report was a mistake. Not to respond would make it appear as if Israel had something to hide. Goodman added, "It is an important thing to be able to defend yourself and to show that you have nothing to hide."

UN Sleeps with War Criminals

The UN is the worst sort of slut. In this chapter we'll look at the slime the UN has crawled into bed with so far.

In 2002 the UN held a World Food Summit in Rome, Italy. The purpose was to formulate a plan that would cut world hunger in half by 2015.

At the summit, the delegates and other representatives were fed a series of "lavish feasts" as reporter Joseph Klein called them.

Six years later, another UN summit was held, a three-day shindig called the "Conference on World Food Security and Challenges of Climate Change." This time the vacuous nature of the organization's scruples plunged to further depths as the invitees included President Mahmoud Ahmadinejad of Iran and President Robert Mugabe of Zimbabwe, men who should be behind bars but instead were protected and coddled by the UN.

Hunger as a Weapon

Mugabe was not a man who sought to prevent hunger. Giving him money to feed his poor was ridiculous. He used hunger as a weapon. One of his regular methods of crowd control was to deny food. During Mugabe's reign, Zimbabwe went from being one of the best-fed nations in that region to one of the worst. The African leader seized acre after acre of farmland from the farmers and turned them into wasteland because Mugabe believed a hungry people didn't fight back so hard.

His crimes were well documented. Take the scheme undertaken by the Zimbabwe government in 2005 known as Operation Murambatsvina, a national eviction and demolition program—another attempt to keep the people too jumpy to become organized.

It was impossible to know the thoroughness of the operation, but it was estimated that hundreds of thousands of Zimbabwe citizens were wiped out in one way or another, whether it was by the destruction of their farmland, deprival of food, or deprival of sanitary water.

Amnesty International found that Mugabe's food and terror programs were most efficient against Zimbabwe's weakest citizens, the million or so AIDS patients, AIDS orphans, children with AIDS, and all the other people who for whatever medical or mental reason could not take care of themselves. The infirm were to be eliminated from the population.

The damage done to Zimbabwe because of Mugabe's sadism was

incredible. The UN knew about this operation—after all, it was revealed by a UN report—yet he had no trouble getting an invite to the three-day party that was a UN food summit.

One Way to Win an Election

Mugabe was, in theory, the elected president of Zimbabwe, but not really. He was a dictator pure and simple. There had once been an election and Mugabe's opponent won. Mugabe declared the election fixed and had his opponent jailed. He let his opponent out of jail soon enough, but with the caveat that any further political ambition on his part, and that meant rallies of any kind, was prohibited.

According to Amnesty International, part of Mugabe's plan included preventing all starvation relief operations from getting a foothold inside Zimbabwe. The law under the dictator prohibited interference in internal business by NGOs.

And it wasn't as if UN delegates weren't vocal about the Zimbabwe holocaust. The UN's under secretary-general for Humanitarian Affairs and Emergency Relief Coordinator, John Holmes, called Mugabe's ban on food a "deplorable decision."

But representatives of the UN fell all but silent in 2008 when Mugabe attended the summit. No one said boo about the fact that he was a mass murderer.

World Hunger? Blame the United States

Did the presentations at the food summit focus on Third World nations and discuss how their brutish leadership contributed to the hunger of their people? Not at all. In fact, at the food conference, the themes of the presentations turned away from struggling nations and focused instead on historically powerful Western countries.

The director of the Food and Agricultural Organization was one speech giver who focused responsibility on the generosity of the rich, say-ing that more money was being spent on climate change than on world hunger and that it should be the other way around. More food (and *more money* for food) needed to be pumped into the starving nations, and more money needed to be poured into those countries in an effort to revitalize the wasted farmland, the director told them.

Clear thinkers, of course, saw through this plan right away. There was no way to ensure that the money went where it said it would. There was no way for the UN to stay with the money. Eventually, the money would be entrusted to a corrupt official who would pocket as much as he could—probably all of it. None would get to the empty plates of the starving.

Stuck with the Tab

That would mean billions of dollars out of American taxpayers' pockets and into the swollen bank accounts of savage dictators such as Mugabe of Zimbabwe. The UN didn't care that the United States already con-tributed billions of dollars every year to combat world hunger. The UN wasn't just asking for thirty billion, it was asking for thirty billion more.

Ahmadinejad Too

But Mugabe's presence at the 2008 food summit was only one of the things that was desperately wrong with that get-together. The other was the presence of Ahmadinejad, who predictably used the global forum to launch verbal salvos at Israel. He called Israel a "fabricated regime" and prognosticated that Israel was "doomed to go."

Addressing the media, when asked about food, the reason they were there, the Iranian dictator blamed the United States and moved to the next question. He eventually blamed all of the world's woes on the West.

The food summit diplomats nodded dumbly and refilled their plates. No one mentioned that the Iranian dictator had made promises he didn't keep during his rise to power in 2005. He said he would use the distribution of Iran's oil wealth to the people to raise the quality of life in Iran drastically. Of course, precisely the opposite occurred. Ahmadinejad wrecked the Iranian economy in his effort to transform Iran into a military power, strong enough to take on the world, if necessary.

Global Blackmail

The very oil wealth that the dictator had promised would go to the people went instead to fund anti-Israel terrorist groups such as Hezbollah and Hamas. Other money went into Iraq where militants were being armed and trained to kill American soldiers.

A tremendous portion of Iran's oil wealth was funneled into its nuclear enrichment program, with the bottom line being global blackmail. In order to fund all these military and foreign policy pursuits, none of the wealth made it to the Iranian people who have reportedly paid a dramatic price. It was estimated that there were as many as 600,000 children begging on the nation's streets.

Ahmadinejad was very good at finding ways to keep his potential internal enemies happy. The religious leaders in Iran who might have opposed him because of the economy, tended to support him because they were seduced by the pseudoreligious context in which Ahmadinejad placed his foreign policy decisions. As Ahmadinejad was media savvy, it was a fact that he considered his image on the global stage a key part of his program. He loved nothing more than a microphone and an audience too frightened to ask him a real question.

And that was just what the UN provided Ahmadinejad when they invited him to the three-day summit. The UN made certain he would not be embarrassed. So when one particular Italian reporter who had guts and liked to ask tough questions of world leaders wanted to attend, at Ahmadinejad's request, that reporter was not granted access to the UN summit.

The UN and Iran's Nukes

In January of 2010 Ahmadinejad proved that he wasn't happy with the favors the UN had done for him. They weren't big enough and he wanted more. The UN had attempted to broker a deal, whereby Iran would still be able to produce nuclear power but would be less likely to build a nuclear bomb. The deal proposed that Iran export its uranium abroad where it would be enriched and returned for use in a Tehran medical reactor.

The Iranian leader went on TV and said he had good news. At a press conference following an address before the Iranian parliament, Ahmadinejad said he had sent the UN a counteroffer and was awaiting its response. He added that "Iran's scientific progress will be a cause of happiness for the Iranian nation and all free nations of the world."

The use of the word "free" can only be seen as ironic, like the actor whose ego is bursting out of his head because he's just won an award, yet calls the experience "humbling." Perhaps when Ahmadinejad said free, he meant precisely the opposite.

The U.S. Ambassador the UN Hated

A lot of American diplomats have been milquetoasts, but not all of them. One recent U.S. ambassador entered the tower of secrets with fists clenched, ready to fight for American interests.

As George W. Bush's ambassador to the UN from 2005 to 2007, John R. Bolton proved to be a forceful advocate of American interests, a powerful voice for UN reform, and a staunch defender of the cause of human rights.

He was a critic of corruption, mismanagement, waste, and inefficiency at a world body that received several billion dollars a year from U.S. taxpayers. He did his best to shake up an institution that had for decades resisted change and cast a revealing light on an elite UN establishment that has long thrived amid a culture of complacency and secrecy.

Bolton's record was outstanding in three key areas: international security, human rights, and UN reform. He dramatically raised the profile of issues from peacekeeping abuses to the UN's need for transparency, accountability, and effectiveness.

Bolton Bio

Bolton was born (1948) and raised in Baltimore. Although he grew up middle class, son of a firefighter, he won scholarships and attended the best schools, finishing his formal education at Yale and Yale Law.

He began his career in conservative politics by running the Students for Goldwater campaign in 1964. While in college, he shared classes with future chief justice of the United States Clarence Thomas. Bolton avoided a Vietnam stint by joining the National Guard, explaining that he considered the war unwinnable. He said he didn't want to "die in a Southeast Asia rice paddy," and didn't want to sacrifice his life to take jungle turf when someday Teddy Kennedy was just going to give it back.

He later went international, making a big career leap from 1997 to 2000 when working pro bono for Kofi Annan's personal envoy to Western Sahara. After a stint as a senior vice president for a conservative think tank, Bolton joined the first Bush administration and worked in a variety of roles for the State and Justice departments, finally serving as general counsel for the U.S. Agency for International Development (USAID).

During the Clinton era, he was the executive director of the Committee on Resolutions in the Republican National Committee. During the second Bush administration, he spent the first term as the under secretary of state for Arms Control and International Security.

He spent years active in the Council on Foreign Relations (CFR), a cutout for secret-society activity that, as we've seen, was largely responsible for the birth of the UN. In 2005 he was appointed as U.S. ambassador to the UN.

Senate Says No

Just being appointed to the UN was an adventure for Bolton. Because of his reputation as a tough-minded and outspoken diplomat, the kind other diplomats hate, George W. Bush tried and failed to get Bolton approved by the U.S. Senate.

Bolton had made provocative statements regarding North Korea—shocking!—and he made the accommodators very nervous. Bolton had been making it clear for years that he couldn't have less respect for the UN. "There is no such thing as the United Nations," he said in 1994.

In 1997 he noted that UN treaties were not law, merely "political obligations." He said that the only countries who believed in international law were those that wanted to constrict America's power.

Not all his criticisms were a hawk's dream, however. He criticized the UN "humanitarian interventions" in Kosovo that were in reality military surges. He said you can't call it humanitarian when what you're really doing is "bombing innocent civilian Serbs into the ground in order that the Albanians can come back and ethnically cleanse the Serb's relatives out of what's left of Kosovo."

When Bush nominated Bolton to be ambassador of the UN, fifty-nine former American diplomats wrote letters asking the Senate to turn him down. When Bolton was not approved by the Senate, Bush was forced to sidestep the process and installed Bolton in the job directly, citing the emergency of wartime.

In 2003 Bolton made the talk-show circuit singing the merits of the war in Iraq. Bolton filled the vacancy created when John C. Danforth resigned as UN ambassador during the autumn of 2004.

UN Ambassador

Bolton was not like your typical ambassador, blue blooded and cocktail tipsy. He looked at his new job and he didn't see party time. He saw before him a septic organization, deformed and disfigured by corruption. He saw an organization with no concept of management. The amount of wasted money and time made Bolton's head spin.

Moreover, he saw the way the United States' power had slipped over the generations at the UN, and he decided for once the UN would get a U.S. ambassador who was willing to speak his mind and who didn't care whose Third World toes he stomped on.

And he did speak up. There was a UN establishment, he said, that thrived on doing nothing, nothing good at least, and doing it in the shadows.

It is largely because of Bolton's efforts that much of the information in this book came to light. He turned the flashlight on the disease-ridden

UN and the free press followed the light. Among the troubles that Bolton exposed were the pattern of sexual abuses committed by UN peacekeepers in war-torn sections of the world.

Bolton the Blunt

His statements regarding misuse of the UN's budget and international power made him the same sort of diplomat that his enemies had feared he would be. He stirred the pot. He told North Korea that it had to stop using "normal relations with the United States" as a lure for U.S. concessions. It was about time, Bolton said, that North Korea realized that the United States just wasn't that into them. We didn't care if we had normal relations with them or not. Such a relationship might've been beneficial to them, but not to us. All we wanted was for them to stop developing their military capabilities so it would be cheaper to defend ourselves against them.

With hawks in the White House, the UN secretary-general said he wanted to give the UN Security Council sole power to determine when and where military aggression could be used. Bolton made it clear the United States would always attack whom we wanted to attack regardless of what the UN said. And that included any nation that supported terrorism, any nation that sought nuclear capabilities, and any nation that attacked Israel.

UN Shortcomings

During his stint as ambassador, Bolton repeatedly testified regarding the UN's shortcomings before Congressional and Senate committees. He didn't just gripe about the UN either. He wasn't just a guy with an encyclopedic knowledge of the UN and a penchant for cleaning house. He got things done as well.

Bolton was responsible for resolutions demanding that North Korea and Iran curb their nuclear programs. He helped construct a peace accord that greatly diminished violence between Israel and Hezbollah.

George W. Bush was thrilled with Bolton's job as UN ambassador, saying, "I know he did a fabulous job for his country. On issue after issue, Bolton delivered."

Truth was, Bolton didn't believe in playing nice with one's enemies, which is practically the theme of the UN Charter. He called them the way he saw them. Because he was a bridge burner, more than a few ambassadors at the UN breathed a big, chest-heaving sigh of relief when Bolton was gone. Said one ambassador, "He sometimes made it very difficult to build bridges because he was a very honest and blunt person. Ambassador Bolton wanted to prove that at the UN nothing works."

Hated by the UN establishment and Democrats, Bolton was denied U.S. Senate confirmation and left the UN in January 2007. He turned his sixteen-month UN stint into a book called *Surrender Is Not an Option*.

Global Warming: The Big Lie

The UN has used the theory of "Global Warming" to milk a lot of money out of the world's more well-to-do countries. Like us. Mostly us. No matter what the UN might plan to do regarding climate change, you know who's getting stuck with the bill.

This debate over why the Earth is warming up, has been a profitable one for the UN, until recently when it has, to a large degree, fallen apart—a crumbling for which they have only themselves to blame.

The theory, to put it in a nutshell, was that the Earth was warming up and the polar ice caps were melting, and the reason for this phenomenon was us—mankind. We have abused our environment and have caused a revolt by Mother Nature that could render us extinct.

If you wanted to sell the theory to the millionaires of the world, you'd have to convince them of two things: one, that global warming was real and was caused by man, and two, that man could "fix it" simply by the very expensive process of "going green."

The human race can be so conceited. If global destruction is on its way, a cataclysm of biblical proportions, do we really believe we can stop it by walking that three blocks to the store or using roll-on instead of aerosol deodorant?

Here is the part they do not want you thinking about: As for global warming, if it exists—and regardless if it is caused by humans or just a cycle in nature—there is no evidence we have any power whatsoever to stop it. If it's true, we're doomed.

Feeling Hot, Hot, Hot

In recent years, the global warming theory was being pushed whole-heartedly by the World Meteorological Organization (WMO), subject of the earlier chapter titled "Nest of Thieves." The WMO reported that the first decade of the twenty-first century was the hottest ever recorded. That sounds pretty scary until you realize they have only been recording the temperatures around the world since 1850.

The report gave the obligatory definition of the problem, calling it the "greenhouse effect," and describing how carbon dioxide (CO_2) and other gasses trapped the heat from the sun. In a natural world, the amount of CO_2 being produced would be matched by the quantity of new oxygen that was a by-product of plants. But our world was out of whack, with carbon dioxide slowly taking over.

Powwow in Copenhagen

In response to the WMO's report, the UN held a conference in Copenhagen, Denmark. The subject was "Controlling Rising Tempera-tures." The previous UN climate-change agreement was the Kyoto Protocol of 1997, which listed changes countries could make to help prevent the steady rise in the world's thermostat.

UN representatives gathered in Copenhagen to update the Kyoto Protocol. World leaders spoke. As is always true when diplomats gather, proposals were at the same time ridiculously vague and specific.

Time was spent determining what fraction of a degree they would set as their goal for maximum annual warming, as if humanskind could slap God's hand away from some global thermostat and manipulate it themselves.

But like the WMO, the UN as a whole knew a moneymaking proposition when it saw one, and once proclaiming that humans had it within their capabilities to save the Earth, they would be compelled to give it their best shot, and that was going to cost a lot of money.

Accord Without Bones from an Organization Without Teeth

The Denmark conference spawned the Copenhagen Accord, a remarkably brief document—only three pages long. The "bare minimum" expectation going into the conference was that a firm deadline for negotiating a binding international treaty would be agreed upon. This was not accomplished—not even close. The conference agreed only to "take note" of the accord, which went unendorsed. Five countries at the conference voted no to "taking note."

Although almost two hundred countries were represented at the conference—and it was the smaller countries that clamored hardest for anti-climate change—the eventual accord was only signed by a few. They were Brazil, China, India, South Africa, and the United States.

Many of the diplomats in Denmark later cried crocodile tears that the Copenhagen Accord was not stronger. Its proclamations were merely suggestions. Each country was to take it upon itself to make sure they were complying with the suggested rules.

But those rules were not law, so there was no way to punish a country for agreeing to the Copenhagen Accord and then reneging when it came to controlling their own emissions. This set up a system whereby the UN could send money to poorer countries to help them comply with the new climate change rules, yet without a process to slow down corruption.

If past UN performance can be any indication, there will be plenty of factories and industrial areas where emissions will stay the same despite the U.S. tax dollars being spent to reduce them.

China Veto

Although China eventually signed the accord, they argued against stronger suggestions. The original proposal called for smaller nations to cut by half the quantity of greenhouse gasses they produced. Large developed nations would have been expected to cut their greenhouse emissions by 80 percent. China used its veto power to nix that notion.

China, largely responsible for passing such a flaccid accord, was quick to sing its praises once the job was done. Chinese premier Wen Jiabao bragged that his country took a major role is shaping the accord.

Desperate Tuvalu

Although for many diplomats, the conference may have just been another opportunity to put on the tux, drink champagne, and have their photos taken while standing beside world leaders, there was at least one diplomat who took matters seriously—whose survival, he felt, would be determined by the fruits of the conference. That was the representative from the tiny South Pacific island of Tuvalu, an island that could become submerged if current trends of warming and melting continued.

Following the conference, the representative cried that it was all such a tragic waste of time. What good were the new UN regulations if the UN could not enforce its new regulations with the power of law?

Coming Apart at the Seams

If there is a saving grace at the United Nations, it is that its anti-American bent is often undone by their ineptitude. The Copenhagen Accord was mostly illusion to begin with but dissolved into pure vapor during the first weeks of 2010.

The plan was for countries to submit to the UN their plans for reducing emissions of climate-altering gasses by January 31, 2010. But with three weeks to go before the deadline, only twenty-four countries had submitted a letter saying that they agreed to the terms of the accord, according to Yvo de Boer, the Dutch official who was the executive secretary of the UN Framework Convention on Climate Change.

Regarding the actual distribution of the $30 billion set aside to help out the countries that would be most affected by climate change, there had been "no progress." Not only was it unclear who was going to receive the money, but it was unclear who was going to donate the money.

Situation Normal

At the same time, even as the accord was revealing itself to be no accord at all, the evidence that had been presented at the conference in support of humanmade climate change turned out to be faulty.

The international scientific panel overseen by the UN to present such evidence announced in January 2010 that they were sorry, but they had (oops) given out some incorrect information. That panel was the UN's Intergovernmental Panel on Climate Change (IPCC).

They had made a few miscalculations, and to make a long story short, they greatly overstated the rate at which the Himalayan glaciers were melting. Their initial report was that at the rate that melt was occurring the glaciers would be gone by 2035. Another stab at the calculator revealed that this date was pessimistic, and the scientist who was supposed to have quoted the 2035 date in the first place denied saying it. Turned out the statistic was based solely on a nonscientific magazine article published in 1999. Whoever was supposed to verify that figure must've called in sick that day. No new date for the disappearance of the glaciers was submitted, but it was noted that "scientists differ" on whether the trend toward melting actually exists and in what way the Himalayan glaciers would be affected. Given that, could it be any surprise that the nations of the world weren't lining up to commit funds to the effort?

Oops Number Two

According to Jonathan Leake, science and environment editor for London's *Sunday Times*, the UN's climate science panel, the IPCC, had "wrongly" linked global warming to the increased numbers of natural disasters as of late.

The claim was caused, the UN panel said, by a misreading of an unpublished report on climate change that pondered a possible connection between climate change and natural disasters. The UN employee doing this research apparently didn't make it to the end of that section when the authors of the paper rejected the link between climate and disasters for lack of evidence. The UN reported it as fact.

The IPCC report, though incorrect, became an instant favorite of those who banged their drums and said the world was coming to an end. It still crops up on cable news, spouted by a self-promoting talking head and represented as fact. At the UN's climate summit in Copenhagen, the climate and disaster link was part of one side's *mantra*.

Implanting the Message on a Word Virus

The ersatz climate and disaster link suggested by the UN's research group crept into the rhetoric of speechmakers, guys like Ed Miliband, Great Britain's energy and climate-change minister, who suggested a 2007 flood in Bangladesh might have been caused by global warming.

Miliband seemed purposefully to ignore existing scientific evidence when he questioned the character of those who believed there wasn't a climate and disaster link. It's a common strategy of conspiracy cover-up artists to ridicule the blurters of truth. Those who didn't get with the program, no matter how illusionary the program, were attacked.

Miliband said, "We must not let the skeptics pass off political opinion as scientific fact. Events in Cumbria give a foretaste of the kind of weather runaway climate change could bring. Abroad, the melting of the Himalayan glaciers that feed the great rivers of South Asia could put hundreds of millions of people at risk of drought. Our security is at stake."

President Obama drank the Kool-Aid! He said that because of global warming, "more powerful storms and floods now threaten every continent." Turn off your mind, relax, and float downstream.

That link was sewn into the conference's collective thought pattern.

There came to be a time, only a couple of years back, when almost three out of four believed global warming was a genuine phenomenon. The global warming lobby did its job well and helped saddle Uncle Sam with a humongous global warming fee. That's the price you pay for being a "rich" country, so say the poor countries with gluttony and hatred in their eyes.

Melting Glaciers

Once the IPCC proved to be so sloppy when it came to the melting of the Himalayan glaciers, every nook and cranny of the report was poked and probed. Research revealed that the IPCC had been *pushing* for a connection between climate change and natural disasters since at least 2007 when it published a report blaming the rise in costs on natural disasters and the natural disasters on global warming.

The claim was later revealed to have come from a 2006 paper written by Robin Muir-Wood, the head of research at Risk Management Solutions in London. And even that paper allowed for the possibility that the extreme weather increase came almost totally in the form of increased hurricane activity—which *had* increased, but not as much as public opinion suggested.

An element of bad luck made the active hurricane season seem even worse than it was. Populous areas had been devastated, creating the feeling that the actual weather increase was greater than it actually was.

Muir-Wood's paper was commissioned by Roger Pielke, an environmental studies professor at Colorado University, for presentation at a conference which, in its summary, said that "there was no evidence" to link global warming with any "increase in the severity or frequency of disasters."

The IPCC quoted the paper selectively to produce the opposite conclusion. Pielke, when he found out about it, was steamed at the IPCC for the way they'd misused his research. He said that it was despicable to cite one small portion of his paper while ignoring the rest of the paper and to eliminate mentioning the rest of the research in the field. It was wrong. They were purposefully pushing an agenda.

When that same IPCC report was republished the following year, a small-print caveat had been added, noting that "we find insufficient evidence to claim a statistical relationship between global temperature increase and catastrophe losses." What would seem like a tremendous shift in policy was deemed worthy of only an asterisk and nary a mention in Copenhagen.

Bum Rap

In response to media complaints over the evidence that wasn't evidence, the IPCC said they were going to gather up all the latest data and write a brand-new report about the possible connection between climate change and natural disasters and extreme weather.

The vice chairman of the IPCC was Professor Jean-Pascal van Ypersele, a climatologist at Louvain Catholic University in Belgium. He was also the global media contact when there was some serious splainin' to do. Here's an example: after the melting-glaciers scandal, he said "despite recent events" the IPCC still went about its business in a "very rigorous and scientific" way.

In 2010 the new cochairman of the IPCC working group overseeing the climate impacts report was Professor Christopher Field, director of the Department of Global Ecology at the Carnegie Institution in California. He said the 2007 report was getting a bum rap. It was a long and detailed report, the great majority of which was true. One mistake in one part and everyone calls the entire report shaky—and that just wasn't true, Field explained.

Was the European Union (EU) put off by the UN's faulty evidence? Not at all. In a statement made in January 2010, the EU said it had full confidence in the UN climate report. The UN apologized for the errors and that was good enough for the EU. It was understandable that the EU was slow to turn on UN climate experts as the EU had already invested a lot of Euros in a plan that *USA Today* called "ambitious and costly" to create Europe as a low-carbon economy.

More Sloppy Science

Professor Field and the EU's advantage in the debate lasted until further evidence of errors surfaced, and then promptly vaporized. In February 2010 Fox News reported that, repeatedly now, the UN's IPCC report revealed itself as propaganda. It utilized "sloppy science" in order to make the point it wanted to make.

Fox noted (with delight) that the IPCC report had already been "lambasted" for inaccuracies—they called the incident "Himalayagate"—and now it was going to get pasted again. It was getting to be a joke. The mistakes weren't just a scandal; they were a "growing scandal."

This time the error had to do with South America's Amazon rain forest. The IPCC scientists claimed 40 percent of the rain forest was threatened by global warming. The figure was questioned by the conservative press and found to be based on a World Wildlife Federation study that had nothing to do with global warming. The study was titled "Global Report on Forest Fires." Turned out, the information found in the forest fire study was "verified" using an article written by a green activist-slash-journalist—and the 40 percent guesstimate was discredited when the IPCC's research techniques came to light.

There were now members of the U.S. government who were not only concerned about the way U.S. tax dollars were being spent, but were surprisingly blunt about what was happening at the UN. They didn't say the IPCC report was filled with mistakes. They said it was filled with lies.

Former staff director for the U.S. Senate's Environment and Public Works Committee Andrew Wheeler said, "If it is true that IPCC has indeed faked numbers regarding the Amazon, or used unsubstantiated facts, then it is the third nail in the IPCC coffin. For years we have been told that the IPCC peer review process is the gold standard in scientific review. It now appears it is more of a fool's gold process." He now had no choice but to question the "underpinnings" of the IPCC report.

Scramblin', Ramblin', Bumblin', Stumblin'

At the IPCC itself, the public relations machine was *scrambling*. "Hommina hommina hommina" as Ralph Kramden used to say. Professor Ypersele, now a callused veteran of defending the report, tried this innovative approach: "I would like to submit that this could increase the credibility of the IPCC, not decrease it. Aren't mistakes human? Even the IPCC is a human institution." Wow, that was a swing and a miss, but a valiant effort to spin the positive out of disaster.

Cable news filled segment after segment with the IPCC weenie roast. A Canadian economics professor said that the UN wanted to sound like it was self-aware and self-correcting in the aftermath of the global warming report crash and burn. But in reality the IPCC hadn't admitted a thing until outside forces investigated it and outed it a as purveyor of propaganda rather than science. The professor said it was time to start over with the global warming research because the current data was unreliable. He said the IPCC committed a "breach of trust."

Biggest Loser

Perhaps the biggest loser in the collapse of UN credibility regarding climate change was Dr. Rajendra K. Pachauri, who, along with U.S. vice president Al Gore, won the 2007 Nobel Peace Prize. Pachauri was the economist-engineer who headed up the IPCC and whose reputation was bitch slapped when that panel's report proved to be hysterical. By February 2010, Senator John Barrasso (R-WY) was calling for Pachauri's resignation.

It wasn't just the faulty report that troubled Pachauri, it was his own behavior as well. According to the *New York Times* (February 9, 2010),

Pachauri was accused of "profiting from his work as an adviser to" foreign banks and New York investment firms.

Pachauri denied the charges, saying that the income was all donated to a nonprofit research center. His critics had an excuse to become vocal. Pielke told the *Times* that he looked at Pachauri's case and saw "obvious and egregious problems." Pielke said that at best Pachauri's behavior was unseemly. Accepting income (no matter how it was spent) from special interests was unacceptable for any diplomat serving as the chairman of a UN panel. It was an indication of impropriety.

Cattle Pastures and Logging

One thing the IPCC reported on was not a lie: the Amazon rain forest was shrinking, and that was a provable fact through satellite images. There could be no argument there. But some pretty smart people thought global warming had nothing to do with that shrinkage.

Czech physicist and former Harvard teacher Luboš Motl said the shrinkage was caused by "social and economic reasons," such as the clearing for cattle pastures, subsistence agriculture, building of infrastructure, and logging.

The IPCC's transparent sloppiness has thankfully cost the supporters of global warming reform. A 2010 poll revealed that 57 percent of people believed that global warming was real, which was down from 71 percent in 2008.

The pro-warming lobby was injured but not dead. On February 1, 2010, the AP reported that according to UN secretary-general Ban Ki-moon's top climate adviser, János Pásztor, the world had taken a first step toward healing itself, but the reduction of greenhouse gasses had not reached the goals set in sandstone in Copenhagen. Those goals were still within reach, however, if only the UN had just—a—lot—more—money.

Erasing the Holocaust

The Holocaust, with a capital H, refers to the systematic, bureaucratic effort by the Nazi government during World War II to exterminate Jews and other targeted groups. But mostly Jews. Millions. It has been said that with genocide comes denial, and that is certainly true in this case, with enemies of Israel and the United States frequently denying that the Holocaust occurred.

Some do it because they believe it, perhaps—but it is largely believed that many do it just because it irks modern-day Jews as well as anyone with respect for human life. When Muslim leaders trash Israel and call Jewish history lies, it is despicable. When such statements are made on the floor of the UN, it is time to quit that organization.

Iranian Conference, 2006

In December 2006 Iran's president Ahmadinejad convened a conference that both questioned the Holocaust's existence and called for the destruction of Israel—proof once again that denying one holocaust can create the negative energy through which another could take place.

U.S. ambassador Alejandro Wolff said that he'd come to expect Iran and other Muslim nations to deny the Holocaust and raise a fist against Israel. It was when denial of the Holocaust came from surprising sources that he became disturbed. Wolff told one reporter, "We are now witnessing so-called scholars, even world leaders, attempting to revise history, masking a more dangerous agenda."

Passover Shout Down

On April 9, 2009, the first day of Passover and the eve of Easter, there was a meeting of a working group scheduled to make a presentation at an upcoming UN conference on racism. The meeting's controversial moment came when the Iranian delegate moved that article 64 of their presentation's text be removed.

That article read, "Recalls that the Holocaust must never be forgotten and in this context urges all UN members to implement General Assembly resolutions 60/7 and 61/255."

One speaker at the meeting was David G. Littman who coincidentally had also been the scheduled speaker in 2005 when his attempt to condemn suicide bombings in the name of God was shouted down by the Islamic contingent in the room. The motion to remove article 64 did not pass, but the very fact that it was made during the Christian and Judaic celebratory holidays was antagonistic.

Ahmadinejad Speech, 2009

During the autumn of 2009, Ahmadinejad spoke before the UN and again ran through his revisionist history. He used "classic anti-Semitic" imagery. His was a simplistic worldview. The United States and Israel were responsible for all the world's problems—end of story.

He didn't limit his anti-Semitic comments to his formal UN speech either. He began to spout off on the subject from the instant he arrived in New York. He said that he had denied there was a Holocaust in the past, and he was going to do it again, and if anyone was angered by that, he saw it as a source for pride.

Ahmadinejad tied the two prongs of his argument together, claiming that the invention of the Holocaust was used to argue in favor of the creation of Israel in the first place. According to the Iranian leader, the Big Lie was necessary in order to shatter Palestine so the Jews could have their own land.

Now Iran was working on a nuclear weapon that could destroy Tel Aviv. As Ahmadinejad would put it, there could be no peace in the Middle East until Israel was gone. With this as the bottom line, Ahmadinejad characterized his message as basically one of peace.

Ahmadinejad loved the controversy his comments caused, especially when he said them inside UN headquarters with the whole world watching. That controversy was a cause for celebration.

Rabbi Marvin Hier, founder and dean of the Simon Wiesenthal Center, who witnessed the speech in person said, "Listening to the words from the rostrum of the United Nations and the applause at its conclusion, I thought I was watching the reincarnation of a young Hitler addressing the Reichstag to the thunderous applause of his followers."

World's Most Notorious Anti-Semite

Ahmadinejad is unquestionably the world's most notorious living anti-Semite. He repeats the mantras that Zionists (1) dominate the financial centers and (2) force political leaders to agree with them to obtain their financial and media support.

The rabbi said he couldn't believe that sixty-five years had passed since the Holocaust, and now members of the U.S. cabinet, present and past, were pushing and shoving for an opportunity to have discussions with a man who "unabashedly calls for the destruction of Israel and believes Auschwitz was a myth."

Netanyahu Rebuttal

Just as shocking, at least to some, was a speech that followed Ahmadinejad's, in which Israeli prime minister Benjamin Netanyahu spoke before the UN General Assembly presenting evidence refuting Ahmadinejad's statements. He held up photos and said, "See? See the skeletal figures of the unfed prisoners? The Holocaust really did occur."

For survivors of the Holocaust and the families of all the concentration camp victims, it was disheartening to hear that the Israeli leader felt it necessary to defend the Holocaust's reality. One Israeli said that he had come to expect politicians to cheapen the memory of the Holocaust by reducing it to a political argument. "But this?" he asked incredulously.

Four Parts

Netanyahu's speech came in four parts. The first part denounced the Holocaust deniers, and they knew who they were. He expressed his shock and horror that Ahmadinejad had been allowed to say what he did at the UN.

In the second part, he used Ahmadinejad's statement to further justify steps to disrupt Iran's nuclear program. He emphasized that if Iran was to develop the capability to build nuclear weapons, Israel wasn't the only country that would have to worry. Truth be known, he said, the whole world would have to worry.

In the third part of his statement, he criticized the UN, in particular the Goldstone Report that accused Israel of committing war crimes by retaliating against Palestinian rocket attacks from the Gaza Strip. Netanyahu reminded the UN that Israel had the right to defend itself. All nations had the right to self-defense.

Finally, Netanyahu discussed peace, reiterating that Israel wanted peace and that Ahmadinejad could not be more wrong when he said there could be no peace in the Middle East as long as Israel existed. Israel did want peace, but not at the expense of its own security. It would always be Israel's contention that "peace and security go hand in hand."

The UN Is a "Terror-Supporting Entity"

In May 2009 the war of words continued. The UN's anti-Semites and the Israel-bashing Goldstone report were on one side of the dispute; on the other side were Israel and its many supporters. Maayana Miskin of the *Israel National News* reported that a terror victims advocacy group known as Almagor was calling out the UN. In fact Almagor called the UN a "terror-supporting entity."

Almagor director Meir Indor explained why he was using that phrase to describe the UN: "The Israeli government and the Justice Ministry should begin a public relations campaign explaining that the UN is becoming systematically anti-Israel and seeks to cause trouble over Israel's struggle against terrorism." He felt the term was justified because he knew of specific incidents in which suspected terrorists refused to give information to Israeli interrogators because they knew they would be supported by the UN and other organizations. "That fact has led to terror attacks," Almagor said, adding that bereaved families were planning to sue UN officials and others who allowed terrorists to withhold information that might prevent future attacks.

The UN and War: Korea and Elsewhere

For a peacekeeping organization, the UN sure does pack some military oomph. Since the end of World War II there hadn't been a war yet that the UN hadn't had its misshapen militaristic mitts on.

The UN's response to such criticisms becomes a broken record. Its efforts were humanitarian—and, of course, humanitarian acts for the masses must be conducted in an orderly fashion, so armed security is required.

Its military strategy is simple. It exists to prolong every war, create maximum military-industrial consumption, and it tries to keep *either* side from winning. Luckily, this last strategic theme was one that it had tackled with a wide range of success and failure.

The template for UN military planning was stamped only a couple of years after the UN's birth. To paint a rosier image, the UN didn't call it a war. It was called a "police action." The press went along with that for a time, but when all was said and done, it went into the history books as the Korean War.

UN and Korea

The Korean War was the first to be fought under the UN banner—the first hot battle of the Cold War. Korea had divided itself into two nations, north and south, much as the United States had during its Civil War. In June 1950 the forces of communist North Korea invaded democratic South Korea in an attempt to unify the Korean peninsula by force. The UN Security Council ruled that the North was the aggressor. (The Soviet delegate was absent from the session, protesting a previous UN ruling.) A UN force was raised. It was composed of U.S. and its allied troops and was commanded by General Douglas MacArthur. On July 10, 1950, MacArthur was named commander in chief, UN Command. This was not to be an all-out war like World War II. The United States and its allies were representing a UN force, and their actions were to be limited, designed to even up the sides rather than conquer North Korea. When MacArthur was deemed too aggressive, he was fired and the UN war went on without him.

Tearing Up the Middle of the Field

The front line moved back and forth, from South Korea into North Korea. At first the Chinese and North Korean forces pushed into South Korea. Eventually, the battle lines stabilized at the 38th parallel. After three years of fighting, the border was put back where it had been before hostilities began, and in 1953, the war was called a draw.

After the war, a fifteen-foot statue of MacArthur was erected at Inchon, South Korea, where UN forces began their retaliatory invasion. The *man* had liberated South Korea twice: once in 1945, as his forces ended a thirty-five year Japanese occupation of the peninsula, and then again in 1950, with the amphibious invasion of Inchon.

But Korea, largely because of UN restrictions, remained divided, with North Korea still a threat to the Western world. Sixty years later, U.S. intelligence collection efforts still focused on North Korea, which of course *costs money.*

More Korean Nukes

During December 2002, North Korea announced that it would resume operations at its Yongbyon nuclear reactor, located fifty miles north of Pyongyang. The former Soviet Union provided North Korea with a five-megawatt reactor. The reactor was completed before being placed in an inactive status because of a 1994 agreement, under which the United States was to provide fuel oil to North Korea.

As mentioned earlier, as the ropes of restriction were tightened around North Korea, these supplies were cut off. North Korea also had two larger reactors. Of concern was that North Korea had in storage approximately 8,000 spent fuel rods. Those contained sufficient plutonium to construct several plutonium nuclear weapons. When operational, the reactors had the capability to produce additional plutonium for nuclear weapons construction. The UN sent "inspectors" into North Korea to observe the reactors.

From Korea to Nam

As mentioned earlier, they didn't stay long. North Korea eventually booted UN inspectors out of the country and disconnected the video surveillance and monitoring equipment in the reactor. Also, North Korea reopened its reprocessing plant which took the spent fuel rods from the reactor, extracting (refining) the weapon-grade plutonium. Without on-site inspectors, the United States used other intelligence collection tools to monitor what North Korea was doing. Satellites conducted some surveillance, but there was no substitute for on-site inspections. Perhaps North Korea's ruler, Kim Jong-il, was trying to force economic concessions from the United States while the United States was seemingly distracted by events in Iraq and Afghanistan. Or maybe it's all a one-way street heading toward global nuclear blackmail.

After the cease-fire in Korea, the UN continued to become a part of every military action, governing the action and picking up the pieces. But they were more subtle about it. By Vietnam the UN no longer waved its banner wide and high. By the 1960s the UN's left-leaning ways made them secretly side with the Communist forces of North Vietnam. The UN had been there when the French fought its Southeast Asian war during the 1950s, and the UN was there when Vietnam became a meat grinder for American boys. And its still there. Today Vietnam is a UN member, and the UN operates one of its international schools in Hanoi.

The UN and the Second Iraq War

It is a fact that global history is too jumpy to predict. The enemy from the last war is just as apt to be the ally in the next. During the Cold War, the United States was opposed to Russia in its Afghanistan adventures. Back in those days, the United States supported the Taliban and even helped supply Osama bin Laden with equipment to help force the Russians out of that country.

A generation later and the United States was "friends" with the Russians in the War on Terrorism, fighting the Taliban and being threatened by bin Laden's al-Qaeda organization. Politics does indeed make strange bedfellows.

The Soviet Union, which had been our number one enemy since the end of World War II, gave up on Communism and became Russia and a group of smaller countries, who were all friendly toward the United States.

The Taliban was known as the government that gave the terrorist group al-Qaeda a home in Afghanistan—and al-Qaeda was the group responsible for the 9/11 attacks. The friend of our enemy is our enemy, and our military and paramilitary forces have spent the last decade trying to wipe out the Taliban.

Another example: During the 1980s a bloody war was fought between Iran and Iraq. We supported Iraq and its leader Saddam Hussein in that conflict. Then Iraq invaded Kuwait and we went to Kuwait's rescue. With a second Bush in the White House, Iraq again became a focal point of American foreign policy.

As we examine the UN's blundering role in the buildup to the U.S. invasion of Iraq, again, we see how the UN is a hypocritical organization, preaching peace yet building war. Although much of the evidence the United States used to invade Iraq was pumped up or false, one claim turned out to be true. Iraq had purposefully yanked the UN weapons inspectors around, methodically taking them from place to place where the weapons of mass destruction weren't.

Change in Tone

The tone of our foreign policy toward Iraq changed as soon as Clinton was replaced by George W. Bush in the White House. Saddam and his weapons of mass destruction were not to be tolerated for much longer.

The UN sent weapons inspectors into Iraq to rout out the weapons, which—of course—were well hidden. Bush, whose father had led the first war against Iraq, would finish the job. Saddam was toast. Bush said he'd change the regime with or without the UN's help and with or without the help of allies. It was a matter of national security.

Great Britain helped. Other allies were hesitant. At the start of 2003, UN weapons inspectors were in Iraq unsuccessfully looking for weapons of mass destruction while the Iraqis seemed reluctant to cooperate. War was inevitable.

The UN was there from the start of the war. And the war was only a few months old when the United States discovered the nature of the UN's game. It was a global organization, and it thought big. Plans were for the UN to *take over* Iraq.

"Administering Iraq"

The plan called for the UN to step in quickly and "administer Iraq" within three months of the war's end. A UN Assistance Mission was going to be established in Baghdad that would oversee the new Iraqi government, after Saddam was ousted. The UN would have been in charge of the postwar hunt for weapons of mass destruction and terrorist cells, the protection of Iraq's energy infrastructure (don't forget the oil), the securing of large cities, the border patrol, and the protection of the Kurds.

The UN was a Trojan horse that would never be allowed in because its benevolent façade would tear away the moment power was gained. Through the UN, countries like France and Russia had ambassadors who *liked* Saddam. Germany and France were not to be allowed to have a say in the administration of postwar Iraq because of their prewar relations with Iraq.

UN: Back in the Saddle

Those countries believed that a ruthless dictator was just what Iraq needed. If the UN took over, they would install a new ruthless dictator in Saddam's place—a dictator who would come marching out of the Trojan horse as soon as it made its way through the gates. Maybe this time, he'd be a *communist*.

Why had those countries been quite so contrary to Saddam's overthrow? Was it because they had sweetheart deals of their own with the man? He might have been ruthless, but that didn't keep them from doing business with him.

During the Bush administration, the United States had the onions to stand up to the UN. We spilled the blood; we would administer. UN plans to take over when the war ended failed, not just because the war didn't end, but also because the United States planned to fill that role—at least temporarily.

Bush fought the UN every step of the way, and as it turned out, it was a mismatch. His years demonstrated how weak the United States could make the UN seem, if we were willing to stand up and fight for what was right.

It looked like the UN was flummoxed there for a second. Then the economy tanked, Republicans lost the White House, and it all fell apart. Obama set a schedule (with a *deadline*) for pulling U.S. troops out of Iraq.

When the deadline comes, Iraq will dissolve into chaos, a feast of anarchy, like Hanoi at the end of the Vietnam War. Control will be achieved by the most ruthless. Don't count out the UN. Their Trojan horse is built and ready to go.

Afghanistan

Afghanistan is a good example of how the UN pours salt into wounds that are just about to heal. The U.S. operation there, launched in the days after 9/11, appeared to be winding down during the first weeks of 2002 when intelligence gathered by a UN monitoring group aggravated the situation.

According to former U.S. military intelligence officer Allan Swenson, the UN monitoring group seemed "almost designed to sustain the edge of terror" that had set the teeth of Americans on edge on 9/11.

The UN group reported that bin Laden's terror network might have nerve gas and short-range missiles capable of carrying warheads. Those weapons, plus popular support among the people of Afghanistan, would give al-Qaeda, it was suggested, a means to an uprising despite being decimated by U.S. air and ground attacks.

The report continued, "Due to the strength of this support, the Taliban and al-Qaeda are likely to remain a threat for some time to come. These missiles may be fitted with conventional, chemical, or nuclear warheads."

"The missiles," the UN intelligence report said, "had a range of forty-five to two hundred miles." It wasn't known if those missiles were operational, and they had no information regarding where the missiles were located.

The report also claimed that the Taliban had Sarin and VX nerve gas projectiles that could be fired with artillery. This UN report remains of major importance in Afghanistan where, as of 2010, the war continues, and those missiles still have not been found.

No-Fly List

The UN played their role in drawing the U.S. military into a more complex mission. Unlike the simplistic previous mission: "Show the world the head of bin Laden." Once drawing us in deeper, the UN demonstrated no favoritism toward the red, white, and blue. In fact, they seemed to be rooting for the other side. Go Taliban, beat Yanks.

The UN's rooting interest even seeped into U.S. Homeland Security. After 9/11 it was a priority of U.S. security to keep everyone associated with the Taliban off commercial airliners. There were about one hundred names on the list. Some were successful, older men and seemingly unlikely terrorists. It was considered beneficial to keep these men on the list anyway because there was strong tactical value in making travel for the enemy as difficult as possible. The list of potential aerial terrorists was long and faulty, yet absolutely esssential. The news loved to report on the redheaded seven-year-old from Indiana who was on the list.

Terrorists were no longer allowed to use commercial airliners as weapons. If Taliban leaders wanted to travel, they would have to fly privately or stay on the ground.

Maintaining safe skies was a good thing, and you'd think that an international organization dedicated to giving peace a chance would support the venture. Instead the UN used its power to remove the names of former Taliban officials from the list.

Goodwill Gesture

The reason the UN wanted the ex-Taliban officials off the list was as a gesture of goodwill, as the UN hoped to broker peace in Afghanistan through discussions. The matter, because of its "diplomatic importance," was rushed to a vote. At first, during debate, it looked like Russia was going to vote on the side of American security and keep the names on the list, but by the time the vote was taken, Russia had turned and the "Taliban diplomats" were allowed on commercial airliners, where they might sit next to you or me.

The U.S. spun this as a good thing. Everything was okay. These men were just *former* enemies. They were safe to fly because they'd switched allegiances and were now on the side of Afghanistan president Hamid Karzai. So, it was cool.

The names came up for review in the first place when Kai Eide, Afghanistan's UN special envoy, appealed to the fifteen-nation council to lift sanctions on the ex-Taliban men because they were "willing to renounce violence and join the peace process."

The men on the list included Wakil Ahmed Muttawakil, ex-Taliban minister of foreign affairs and Abdul Hakim Monib, a former Taliban official turned Afghanistan governor.

If this reasoning could be followed, we could save billions of dollars by making all domestic commercial airline passengers take an oath of allegiance to the United States before boarding. The terrorists would refuse and thus give themselves away.

One-Way Deal

This specific instance of allowing formerly forbidden men to fly again, it was revealed, was part of a pattern by the UN to undermine U.S. security. Richard Barrett, chairman of a UN panel that oversaw the implementation of anti-Taliban, anti-al-Qaeda sanctions, said this was desirable because those who turned on the enemy and became our friend needed to be rewarded for that shift in allegiance. They deserved the opportunity, Barrett explained, to play "a full part in the future of Afghanistan."

There were Americans who supported the UN position. A high-ranking

official with the dove group, The United States Institute of Peace, named
J. Alexander Thier, said that anything that worked toward a political rec-
onciliation with the Taliban leadership, former or current, was desired.
"Taking some names off the sanctions list is like a prisoner exchange, a
small step and sign of good faith on the part of UN Security Council
members," Thier said.

They forgot one thing: In a prisoner exchange, both sides get something they want. In this case, the UN made sure the U.S. got nothing—
except a no-fly list with fewer names on it.

Outspoken Eide

Even as he was lobbying for the United States to shorten its no-fly list,
envoy Eide hammered away at U.S. policy along other fronts. He called
for the release of some detainees who were held in Afghan military
prisons.

In true UN fashion, Eide insisted the only road to peace was conversation. The United States, he said, should concentrate on finding the guy
who was *actually in charge* of the Taliban and talk turkey. His statement
implied there might be pretenders to the Taliban-leadership role.

It was acknowledged even by the hawkiest hawk that the endgame in
Afghanistan involved some form of negotiation with what was left of the
Taliban. The United States had no intention of bombing Afghanistan into
oblivion and then planting an American flag in the rubble.

The simplest counterargument against peace talks in early 2010 was
that it was too early. The best rebuttal was to point out that the Taliban,
regardless of whom their real leader was, wasn't ready to talk and wouldn't
be ready until sufficiently humbled by the U.S. military.

What goes unspoken is that the United States, when it does sit down to
talk peace, is going to want to call the shots, to negotiate from a superior
position, and to force the Taliban (or again what is left of it) to bow before
U.S. demands.

Hammer and Anvil

When Obama announced a military buildup and eventual surge into Afghanistan, voices from the UN howled with protest, claiming escalation of hostilities would in the end delay rather than speed up U.S. withdrawal.

According to Robert Naiman, writing for *The Huffington Post*, the analogy that works best is that the best way to squash the Taliban is for the United States to be a sledgehammer and for Pakistan to be the anvil. Trouble is, the United States wields a mean sledgehammer, but Pakistan is a lousy anvil. When the United States swings, the enemy runs for cover across the border into Pakistan.

Only when Pakistan is willing to launch an offensive of its own, pushing the Taliban back into Afghanistan, will U.S. military probably muster the decimation necessary for the Taliban to come to a peace table in the properly humble frame of mind.

United States Fights Back

Although the free press has, in some sectors, covered and investigated the UN thoroughly, the mainstream press still has a long way to go. The great majority of Americans still think of the UN in the same benevolent terms they learned in grade school.

The things we know come largely via the slam-bang world of U.S. intelligence. In 2008, near the end of the second Bush administration, the government gathered five hundred documents, consisting of thousands of pages, all damaging to the UN, and put them online. They were classified as For Everyone's Eyes Only.

It was during the release of this treasure trove of information that we first learned of the UN bribes, sex crimes, and fraud. And America started to see the light. I hope this book will be a catalyst for enlightenment. Political corruption in the UN knows no bounds, and we have finally seen the UN for what it is, an enemy of the United States.

The Obama Era

To put it bluntly, President Barack Obama has repeatedly demonstrated an unwillingness to stand up to the United States' enemies. And why? To hush the noise, to make others like us, and to make friends and influence nations. And his coolness toward foreign policy *has* reduced the volume of anti-American noise from around the world. Not that that is going to get us anywhere.

He has also sung the praises of the UN. Obama says the UN should have a greater role in global issues, a song the UN had not heard from an American leader in a while.

That must have been a happy, happy day for the "Loathe America Club." Obama preached a dreamy multilateralism—playing right into the UN's hands. We can only hope that the results are not disastrous.

One hundred days into the Obama administration, during the spring of 2009, after Obama was harshly criticized for behaving civilly toward Latin American leaders during a trip to that region, Presidential advisor David Axelrod said, "I think what has happened is that anti-Americanism isn't cool anymore." Axelrod was addressing a conference hosted by the Religious Action Center, a Reform Judaism organization that sought to influence society and politics. "I had the honor and the pleasure to travel with Obama to Europe recently, to the G20 conference, and to NATO and to the EU and, finally, to Turkey and Iraq," Axelrod went on. "It was an extraordinary experience not just to see the way world leaders received

Obama but to see the way average citizens in these various countries received him."

For the UN there were tangible benefits immediately in terms of more money. The United States started paying all its bills again.

Axelrod represented an administration that had bought the UN's grifter gab full throttle. When the UN rubbed its thumb over its forefinger, the United States pulled out its wallet!

Axelrod said, "We pushed hard for more money for the IMF so we could help struggling economies, more money for impoverished and developing nations who are having such a hard time, food security programs, all this came out of the G20 and the United States played a huge role in that."

Regarding Obama's resetting of foreign policy around the world and especially in the Middle East, Axelrod said, "When you look at the fact that the Cubans for the first time are saying we are willing to talk about democracy, human rights, and political prisoners.... When you look at the fact that Chavez has said we want to talk about returning ambassadors and restoring relationships, these are first steps. We are not naïve. We know there is a long way to go...but I believe we have made great progress."

Some might call that, not progress, but retreat.

Help!

On Wednesday, September 23, 2009, Obama spoke before the UN and, like Bush before him, he called for help. He told the assembly that the United States couldn't solve all the world's problems alone. Solving global crises, he said, "cannot be solely America's endeavor."

The speech came as the climax of a whirlwind week of diplomacy. The president attended international meetings regarding climate change, the Middle East, and the global economy—all while being scrutinized by the American media regarding his plans for the war in Afghanistan.

Liberals appreciated the return to civility. Though Obama's call for help reminded some of Bush, Obama was doing his best—for what it was worth—to change the tone between the United States and the rest of the world, to make nice, something his predecessor had not found necessary.

There was conservative resistance at home to anything resembling appeasement. Many worried that Obama would make too nice—like announcing a schedule with dates for the withdrawal of U.S. military forces from Afghanistan. He gave away the store. The plan, clearly, was to thaw all those many unfriendly nations. But would it have any effect? The very nations who were the frostiest also had the longest memories. Iran was still angered at the memory of a U.S.-sponsored coup d'etat in that country fifty years ago.

Deadline for Withdrawal

For those who didn't notice the change in tone, Obama pointed it out. No one could miss his commitment to reduce the "reflexive anti-Americanism, which too often had served as an excuse for our collective inaction."

He called for a "new era," one in which the United States got along with other nations. He said there were reasons to take his olive branch seriously. With his administration came "no more torturing." The detention center at Gitmo was closing. The war in Iraq was winding down. He called for a "global response to global challenges."

And the act went over well. The delegates gave Obama sincere applause. But as was true in America as well, the UN jury was still out on Obama. He might have had a mild and soothing message and manner of speaking, but as his eventual decision to escalate the war in Afghanistan demonstrated, he did not want to appear weak and was prepared to use his military as an avenging weapon. The deadline for the start of withdrawal in Afghanistan, summer of 2011, could have been an empty promise, never mentioned again or formally removed because of new circumstances on the ground.

There was tough talk even in Obama's "make nice" speech at the UN.

Obama called out Iran and North Korea for their refusal to cooperate with international antinuclear proliferation efforts. He said the nuclear programs of those two countries "threaten to take us down this dangerous slope," making our planet a less secure place.

Popular in Africa

Indicative of Obama's effectiveness among African leaders, much of which comes intrinsically because of his skin color and heritage, was Moammar Ghaddafi of Libya, once America's sworn enemy, who now gushed over Obama, saying he was proud that this "son of Africa" was the U.S. leader. He said he would be happy if Obama remained U.S. president forever.

However, when it was Ghaddafi's turn to speak at the UN, he railed against the United States as much as ever. He spoke for an hour and a half about what he felt was excessive American and Western power in the world and the UN. He complained of the UN's "feudal" order in which poor countries were terrorized by the rich and powerful ones, terrorized with UN sanctions and military action.

"It should not be called the Security Council, it should be called the Terror Council," Ghaddafi said.

To his credit, he did not call for Israel's destruction. He said that Israel had a right to exist, even to exist in peace and security. He did say that the Palestinians had legitimate claims and rights, and that the U.S. commitment to Israel was only tolerable if Israel recognized the rights of Palestinians in return—an Obamaesque utopian compromise and daydream.

Fraud and Mismanagement

During the Obama administration, UN fraud and mismanagement continued to be unearthed on a regular basis. In 2010, George Russell reported for Fox News that between 2004 and 2008 the U.S. Agency for International Development (USAID) gave $330 million to that little-known UN agency the Office for Project Services (UNOPS) to develop aid projects in Afghanistan.

The money, of course, didn't provide much Afghanistan aid, but it did pad many pockets up and down the money line. Even as reports of fraud, lack of control, and mismanagement came flooding in, the UNOPS looked the other way. In addition to the USAID contributions to the effort, another $100 million was given to the UNOPS by other U.S. agencies and departments.

There was evidence that at least some of the fraud was premeditated because the bylaws of the UN office were written so as to make it near impossible for future inspectors to examine its books.

A UN investigation into the handling of UNOPS funds was conducted by the Government Accountability Office (GAO), which said that it was pretty sure the USAID funds were skimmed into oblivion, but specific incidents were hard to come by because UNOPS accounting records were so hard to come by.

In conclusion, there was a promise that there were going to be changes, hopefully, in UNOPS, and that all those money leaks were going to be plugged up. In 2010, the GAO still had no way to verify that new rules and money controls were implemented. The office's books were still kept under lock and key where inspectors couldn't get to them.

Skyrocketing Afghanistan Budget

In 2010 the UN's budget for Afghanistan projects was growing rapidly—a quarter of a billion dollars for 2010. With Obama's sizable yet temporary military buildup in that nation, the UN sensed there was going to be plenty of work to do along that front. About a quarter of that was U.S. money.

Obama's plan was to create both a military and civilian surge in Afghanistan so that even as the U.S. military went after the Taliban more aggressively, so would a surge of UN personnel with developmental aid.

And so the quantity of cash flowing through that leaky pipeline to Afghanistan would swell. But will any more money actually make it to its intended goal, or will the pockets of the skimmers continue to be over-stuffed?

There is little reason to believe that things aren't "situation normal" for the UNOPS, just another indication that U.S. interests will continue to be banished to an Afghan outhouse.

Self-Police Shrinkage

During the first Obama year, the UN budget allotted to investigating its own fraud shrank. The UN could no longer afford to self-police, not that their self-policing techniques were ever that effective. But now the internal affairs department would be nonexistent.

An AP report from January 2010 said that the decrease in budget was going to force many cases of UN impropriety to be shelved. That brought happiness to the UN's white-collar criminals.

Trusting any company with investigating itself is foolish. An independent investigator should always be in charge, but trusting the UN with such a chore is just silly. The UN does not want to discover its own mis-management and fraud. That would come too close to confronting the organization's genuine raison d'être. Those shelved cases involved mil-lions of dollars of possible theft and misuse. Five of the dropped cases were in Afghanistan, Iraq, and Africa.

The UN's special anticorruption unit, set up to self-monitor after the Oil-for-Food scandal, was being discontinued for lack of funds. The Pro-curement Task Force had its most effective years between 2006 and 2008 when it reportedly uncovered at least twenty major schemes involving the misuse of more than one billion dollars in UN contracts and foreign aid.

In 2009 cases formerly investigated by the Procurement Task Force were transferred to the UN's do-nothing Office of Internal Oversight Ser-vices, where results figured to be exponentially slower. Fox News noted in January 2010 that more than a year had passed since the UN had completed investigating a case involving its own internal corruption. Self-policing went from tortoiselike to motionless, using empty pockets as an excuse. In the meantime the foreign-aid budgets that were being skimmed were healthier than ever. Investigators employed by the old UN self-policing units were laid off. When the task force disbanded, it handed ninety-five investigations to Oversight and all were promptly discontinued.

According to Nancy Boswell, the president of Transparency International-USA, an anticorruption watchdog organization, "One year after the Procurement Task Force was terminated, it is deeply troubling that allegations persist that the Office of Internal Oversight Services has not vigorously pursued open cases, that its leadership has not put in place a permanent head of investigations, and that it may be narrowing its scope of inquiry."

Among the investigations halted by the budget cuts was one in which one million dollars a day were reportedly leaking from a UN project in Kabul. There were two others. One in Afghanistan that involved evidence of an American firm padding its charges to the UN by more than a million dollars and the other diverting from funding for Afghan elections, roads, schools, and hospitals. Also halted was an investigation into $350,000 in UN funds, designated to start up a radio station for women in Baghdad that ended up helping a white-collar thief pay back a personal loan.

Investigations into some cases were far along when the plug was pulled. For example, a case involving UN collusion and bid rigging was at a point where prosecution was recommended. The case involved a transport company in Africa that had UN contracts steered toward one preferred company, in particular two senior officers. The task force dissolved and no prosecution took place. Another case that was dropped involved $200 million in transportation contracts for UN peacekeeping throughout Africa.

Fox News learned that the discontinuation of these investigations was not simply a matter of budget. In many cases, political pressure was brought to bear before the investigations were discontinued. The budget problems merely supplied a good excuse for that discontinuation.

Even when the task force was in business, its activities were hindered. Businessmen from Russia and Singapore in particular were vocal about their displeasure with the task force and its pesky investigations.

The Government Accountability Project (GAP), a Washington-based nonprofit law firm, looked into the situation and discovered the plain truth. The UN, the GAP said, quashed its own task force, buried its cases, and retaliated against an investigator, in one case, who was trying to protect his investigation's computer files.

The task force had employed investigators who were experts at detecting and stopping white-collar crimes, including Robert Appleton, a former U.S. federal prosecutor. The investigations, when they were still active at all, were then put in the hands of "Oversights Services," where the offices were strangely empty.

Kim for Cash

In March 2007 Claudia Rosett exposed a UN scandal on the other side of the globe, writing about how the UN Development Program (UNDP) office in North Korea was handing money directly to Kim Jong-il, which became known as the Kim-for-Cash scandal.

She exposed how the Korean leader had sponsored efforts to counterfeit U.S. banknotes and launder that money into world markets. The UNDP apparently was paid off in counterfeit $100 bills.

According to Rosett, the UN officials knew that the cash was counterfeit, but instead of reporting this international crime, they put the cash quietly in a safe in their Pyongyang office.

Haitian Vanity Parade

This time Rosett's work pulled the little boy's finger of bias out of the information dyke. As the second year of the Obama administration got under way, there were daily stories in mainstream newspapers getting the word out regarding UN corruption. In many cases, the news was immediate. The effect of our sophisticated communication systems was more apparent than ever when the tragic earthquake in Haiti in 2010 opened up a new venue for UN corruption and ineptitude. Instantaneously, with the speed of an electron, the UN came under fire for its tepid response to a red-hot emergency.

Less than two weeks after Haiti was broken, Guido Bertolaso, the head of Italy's Civil Protection Agency, told RAI television in Italy that he had personally observed the UN's efforts in the disaster area.

"It was a vanity parade," he said. "It was a pathetic situation which could have been much better organized. We are missing a leader, a coordination capacity that goes beyond military discipline."

While he was at it, Bertolaso criticized the U.S. military saying that at times it looked as if Haiti had been invaded and occupied rather than being the beneficiary of a humanitarian effort of tremendous proportions.

Condemning Secret Detention

Even with Obama's overall softening of the United States' image abroad, the UN continued to make it clear that it didn't approve of U.S. behavior. They found our foreign policy (which was, after all, leadership of the free world) heavy handed.

On January 27, 2010, a UN human rights group, instead of going after myriad human rights violations being committed by the barbaric countries of the Third World, set its sites on the United States.

Again.

On that day the so-called investigatory committee released a 226-page report stating that the "secret detention"—that is, location unknown—of so-called terrorists violated International Human Rights Law. Some detainees, alleged terrorists, captured by the United States, were shipped to other countries where methods of interrogation that were more sophisticated were legally available.

Although there were some discussions of poor American behavior before 2001, the great bulk of the report covered U.S. behavior since the War on Terror began on September 11, 2001.

A UN spokesperson explained, "We firmly believe that no matter how legitimate the grounds for detaining someone, there exists no right to conceal the person's whereabouts."

The UN and Taliban Connection

The UN, in its role as a peacekeeping force, as a postoccupation wanna-be, sought to hasten a halt to U.S. military operations in Afghanistan—operations that were undeniably justifiable, the direct result of the 9/11 attacks as well as other terrorist attacks around the world.

The UN's efforts became more persistent and direct after the escalation of grueling mountainous warfare in Afghanistan. The negotiators didn't represent U.S. interests in any way. The fact that we'd been attacked went unmentioned. The UN negotiators sided with the Taliban. It was Kai Eide again in the news, the same guy who had worked to have the names of "former" Taliban officials removed from the no-fly list. Now Eide was having meetings, mano a mano, with Taliban leadership in hopes of instigating "peace talks."

"No offense UN, but stay the hell out of it," was what Americans said. "We're looking for Osama bleepin' bin Laden."

The Eide and Taliban powwow was held. The U.S. government could only gasp and assign a spokesperson. "[Eide] wanted to test for himself the mindset of the Taliban leaders," Secretary of State Hillary Clinton said.

Clinton said that Eide had briefed her about what occurred during the meeting, although she did not know the precise location or time of the meeting or precisely who was in attendance. She appeared unconcerned that something horribly wrong was going on here.

The story was that the Taliban wanted an immediate American withdrawal, and the UN was insisting that the Taliban give up their alliance with al-Qaeda. So the talks didn't get very far. But was that the real story?

Moolah

Best guess is that much of the meeting concerned money. The insurgents in Afghanistan, the UN believed, could be bought—that if the bribes were large enough, they would quit their insurgency and magically transform into law-abiding Afghan citizens.

The notion could not have been more naïve. You give money to the terrorists, and you create rich terrorists, those who can afford to buy better weapons and carry out larger and more complex terrorist operations.

Which aspect of the UN's enemy status was stronger? Was it the ideological part that hated the United States and Israel or the corrupt part that diverted the money flow from your wallet to a man training suicide bombers on the other side of a mountain from U.S. troops?

Was it possible that the UN would be willing to sell out the United States, not because of hatred, but because it was a way for the monetary vampires to make a buck, a way to start a new money flow to drain? You bet. For the UN, that was killing two birds with one stone.

Engaging the Taliban as If They Were Equal Partners

There was naturally a concern that Eide's ill-advised UN negotiations with the Taliban would undermine United States military operations there. That concern came not just from the U.S. but from the official Afghan government as well.

Daniel Korski, former adviser to the Afghan government and member of the European Council on Foreign Relations (CFR), said that Afghan leaders did not trust the UN to negotiate with the Taliban. Korski said, "It's not trying to break up the insurgency by hollowing it out but rather engaging them as if they were equal partners in a peace process."

Korski feared that the UN negotiations would lead to unacceptable circumstances and that concessions would be made. Afghanistan might get a new constitution. There might be a power-sharing agreement to appease the insurgent tribal leadership.

The Taliban had a lot of support from many UN member nations. They were, after all, fighting and killing Americans. Not all the support for the UN actions came because the United States was the enemy. Some anti-American sentiment had pragmatic roots and featured pessimistic yet feasible prognostications. Those voices argued that the military battle, for the United States, was not winnable. As was revealed with such horror during World War II in Italy, fighting in the mountains was very hard, too hard for invading forces to advance. What the United States needed, they believed, was an exit strategy, and that was what the UN was working on when they met with Taliban leadership.

The Taliban denied that any meeting with the UN ever occurred. Eide was not telling the truth, they said. The Taliban said it was composed of fighters, not talkers. In reality, the Taliban didn't need to be aggressive. It already had a deadline for the start of U.S. withdrawal from Obama, summer of 2011. And the UN wanted to open bribing season. There was no reason for the Taliban to do anything other than wait for the United States to leave and return to business as usual (only now with some UN cash to bolster its power).

Summing Up

So in conclusion, we have established several key points about the truly terrifying combination of sinister and vacuous that can be found in that tower of secrets overlooking the East River.

The UN is corrupt, with all flows of money subject to skimming or diverting. We give it money to help feed the poor and fix disasters, and the cash ends up in some crook's pocket.

UN personnel have a history of vice and perversion, replete with a barbaric view of females and children. In country after country, UN employees are involved in human trafficking and pedophilia.

The UN started out as a pro-Illuminati organization, one with complex but ultimately foolish plans for a perfect future world, but it was overtaken during the last generation by the Islamic bloc.

The mindset at the UN as of 2010 was that the United States and Israel were responsible for all the world's ills. Once they gained inclusion in the UN, the Islamic countries stuck together on issues but then galvanized to form a rigid wall between the UN and almost any Western interest. At one UN gathering, Iran's lunatic leader Ahmadinejad went to the podium and accused the Western powers of being pretentious, of believing themselves to be "rulers of the world."

Another malevolent force within the UN is supplied by the banana dictators Hugo Chavez and Fidel Castro, who represent a surprisingly strong bloc of leftists left over from the Cold War. The UN has legitimized them by providing them forums for their madness. Chavez called an American leader "the Devil" and referred to the Western powers as the "imperialistic empire."

The insidious anti-American forces in the UN bully and take advantage of the world's poor and stricken nations that fall in line with the Islamic bloc. The result, an organization that is a Pisa-like slant away from us. "There is now a sense of the oppressed versus the oppressor," explained one U.S. official. Countries cluster, their cohesion composed of Third World similitude and hatred for the United States.

And that's the way it's always going to be. Why the hell are Americans paying for it?

Bibliography

Books

Babbin, Jed. *Inside the Asylum: Why the United Nations and Old Europe Are Worse Than You Think*. Washington, DC: Regnery Publishing, 2004.

Benson, Michael, Danny O. Coulson, and Allan Swenson. *The Complete Idiot's Guide to National Security*. Indianapolis, IN: Alpha Books, 2003.

Bolton, John. *Surrender Is Not an Option: Defending America at the United Nations*. New York: Threshold Editions, 2007.

Browder, Earl. *Victory: And After*. New York: International Publishers, 1942.

Bunson, Matthew. *The Pope Encyclopedia: An A to Z of the Holy See*. New York: Crown Trade Paperbacks, 1995.

Coleman, John. *Conspirators' Hierarchy: The Story of the Committee of 300*. Carson City, NV: America West, 1992.

Cumings, Bruce. *The Origins of the Korean War*. Vol. 1, *Liberation and the Emergence of Separate Regimes*. Princeton, NJ: Princeton University Press, 1981.

Gold, Dore. *Tower of Babble: How the United Nations Has Fueled Global Chaos*. New York: Three Rivers Press, 2005.

Hammer, Richard. *The Vatican Connection*. New York: Charter Books, 1982.

Harris, Neil. *Understanding Drugs: Drugs and Crime*. London, England: Aladdin Books, 1989.

Israeli, Raphael. *Islamikaze: Manifestations of Islamic Martyrology*. London, England: Frank Cass, 2003.

Jasper, William F. *Global Tyranny Step by Step: The United Nations and the Emerging World Order*. Appleton, WI: Western Islands, 1992.

Keith, Jim, ed. *The Gemstone File*, Atlanta, GA: IllumiNet Press, 1992.

Klein, Joseph A. *Global Deception: The UN's Stealth Assault on America's Freedom*. Los Angeles, CA: World Ahead, 2005.

Perloff, James. *The Shadows of Power: The Council on Foreign Relations and the American Decline*. Appleton, WI: Western Islands, 1988.

Powell, Jillian. *Crimebusters: Drug Trafficking*. Brookfield, CT: Copper Beech Books, 1997.

Prados, John. *Keeper of the Keys: A History of the National Security Council from Truman to Bush*. New York: William Morrow, 1991.

Shawn, Eric. *The UN Exposed: How the United Nations Sabotages America's Security and Fails the World*. New York: Sentinel, 2006.

Still, William T. *New World Order: The Ancient Plan of Secret Societies*. Lafayette, LA: Huntington House, 1990.

Swenson, Allan, and Michael Benson. *The Complete Idiot's Guide to the CIA*. New York: Alpha Books, 2003.

Periodicals and the Internet

"Ahmadinejad's UN Speech Confirms Him as World's Most Dangerous Anti-Semite." *www.iranholocaustdenial.com* (posted September 25, 2008, accessed January 19, 2010).

Baker, Peter, and Glenn Kessler. "UN Ambassador Bolton Won't Stay." *The Washington Post*, December 5, 2006.

Bavier, Joe. "UN Congo Troops Traded Arms for Gold-Rights Groups." *www.reuters.com* (posted May 23, 2007, accessed January 29, 2010).

Beichman, Arnold. "UN Fraud on Terror." *www.washingtontimes.com* (posted April 19, 2004, accessed January 6, 2010).

"The Beneficiaries of Saddam's Oil Vouchers: The List of 270." *United Press International* dispatch, January 29, 2004.

Brewer, Jerry. "Cold War Espionage Is As Hot As Ever." *www.scribd.com* (posted December 25, 2006, accessed January 18, 2010).

Broder, John M., and Elisabeth Rosenthal. "UN Official Says Climate Deal Is at Risk." *New York Times*, January 20, 2010.

Chesterman, Simon. "The Spy Who Came in from the Cold War: Espionage and International Law." Paper presented before the American Political Science Association, August 31, 2006, Philadelphia, PA. *www.allacademic.com* (accessed January 18, 2010).

Clayton, Jonathan, and James Bone. "Sex Scandal in Congo Threatens to Engulf UN's Peacekeepers." *London Times*, December 23, 2004.

Coomaraswamy, Radhika. "Girls in War: Sex Slave, Mother, Domestic Aide, Combatant." *www.un.org* (posted January 1, 2009, accessed January 11, 2010).

Cornwell, Rupert. "My Fantasy Head of the United Nations." *www.independent.co.uk* (posted September 23, 2006, accessed January 6, 2010).

Cowell, Alan. "Britain Acts to Expel Muslim Firebrands." *International Herald Tribune*, July 21, 2005, p. 1, 5.

"Criticism of Suicide Bombers Censored at the UN." International Humanist and Ethical Union website. *Iheu.org* (posted July 26, 2005, accessed December 29, 2009).

Dan, Uri. "Blown Away: Israel Kills Hamas Chief in Gaza Raid." *New York Post*, March 22, 2004, p. 1.

Darnton, John. "Union, but Not Unanimity, as Europe's East Joins West." *New York Times*, March 11, 2004, p. A1.

Davies, Dave. "After the Cold War, Russian Espionage in the U.S." *www.npr.com* (posted January 30, 2008, accessed January 18, 2010).

Davis, Ian, and David Isenberg. "The Long History of UN Espionage." Global Policy Forum. *www.globalpolicy.org* (posted March 8, 2003, accessed January 18, 2010).

Doughty, Bob, and Faith Lapidus. "Revisiting the Accord from Copenhagen." Voice of America website. *www1.voanews.com* (posted and accessed January 19, 2010).

"EU Backs Climate Change Report Despite Flaws." *USA Today*, January 27, 2010.

Farnham, Nicholas. "Taking Withdrawal from UNESCO Seriously." *Comparative Education Review*, February 1986, p. 148.

Farrell, Steve. "The UN-American United Nations." *www.newsmax.com* (posted 1999, accessed January 21, 2010).

Filkins, Dexter. "UN Mission Head in Afghanistan Met with Taliban Envoys." *New York Times*, January 29, 2010.

Fitzgerald, Hugh. "Stop Taking the UN Seriously." *www.jihadwatch.org* (posted December 9, 2005, accessed December 30, 2009).

Gabriel, Dana. "Dusting Off the UN Law of the Sea Treaty." *www.border firereport.net* (posted March 19, 2009, accessed January 27, 2010).

Gardiner, Nile. "Limit the Role of the United Nations in Post-War Iraq." *www.heritage.org* (posted April 1, 2003, accessed March 29, 2010).

——————, and Brett D. Schaefer. "John Bolton: An Effective Force for U.S. Interests at the United Nations." *www.heritage.org* (posted November 17, 2006, accessed March 29, 2010).

Glazov, Jamie. "The Un-PATRIOT-ic Left." *www.frontpagemagazine.com* (posted May 18, 2004, accessed December 16, 2009).

Heilprin, John. "UN Says Nations' Greenhouse Gas Pledges Too Little." *Washington Post*, February 1, 2010.

Henriques, Diana B. "Supplier Accused of Bribes for UN Contracts." *New York Times*, January 22, 2010.

Holt, Kate, and Sara Hughes. "UN Staff Accused of Raping Children in Sudan." *London Telegraph*, January 2, 2007.

"Investigative Reporting Project." Foundation for Defense of Democracies website. *www.defenddemocracy.org* (posted and accessed January 6, 2010).

"Israel Submits Report Rejecting UN Charges of War Crimes." *www1.voanews.com* (posted and accessed January 30, 2010).

"Italian official calls Haiti earthquake relief effort 'pathetic.'" *www.examiner.com* (posted and accessed January 25, 2010).

"Judge Tosses UN Sex Harassment Suit, Citing Immunity." *www.foxnews.com* (posted April 30, 2008, accessed January 12, 2010).

Kennedy, Paul. "Weak States and Scofflaws Have No Business on the Security Council: It's time for the UN to Take Its Most Important Body Seriously." *Wall Street Journal*, October 17, 2008.

Kilgannon, Thomas P. "The UN's Alliance of Anti-Americanism." *www.freedomalliance.org* (posted February 23, 2007, accessed February 1, 2010).

Kirkpatrick, Melanie. "The UN's North Korean Chutzpah." *Wall Street Journal*. June 12, 2008.

Klein, Joseph. "Denying Reform at the UN Human Rights Council." *www.frontpagemag.com* (posted June 3, 2009, accessed December 17, 2009).

——————. "Let's Become 'Deadbeat' on the UN." *www.frontpagemag.com* (posted March 18, 2009, accessed December 22, 2009).

——————. "Moral Poverty at the UN." *www.frontpagemag.com* (posted June 9, 2008, accessed February 1, 2010).

——————. "Pennsylvania Schools Reject Indoctrination." *www.frontpagemagazine.com* (posted March 1, 2006, accessed January 20, 2010).

——————. "The UN Bailout of Hamas." *www.frontpagemagazine.com* (posted January 13, 2009, accessed December 17, 2009).

——————. "The UN-holy Alliance." *www.frontpagemag.com* (posted February 27, 2009, accessed December 22, 2009).

——————. "The UN's Gravy Train to Iran." *www.frontpagemagazine.com* (posted June 17, 2008, accessed December 22, 2009).

Koprowski, Gene J. "UN's Global Warming Report Under Fresh Attack for Rainforest Claims." *www.foxnews.com* (posted and accessed January 28, 2010).

"Korean Arrested on Oil-for-Food Scandal Charges." *www.msnbcnews.com* (posted January 6, 2006, accessed January 7, 2010).

"Kosovo UN Troops 'Fuel Sex Trade.'" *news.bbc.co.uk* (posted May 6, 2004, accessed January 12, 2010).

Kushner, Arlene. "Rockets Fly, the UN Lies." *www.frontpagemagazine.com* (posted December 2, 2008, accessed December 15, 2009).

Leake, Jonathan. "UN Wrongly Linked Global Warming to Natural Disasters." *www.timesonline.com* (posted and accessed January 24, 2010).

"Liberia Sex-For-Aid 'Widespread.'" *news.bbc.co.uk* (posted May 8, 2006, accessed January 13, 2010).

Littman, David G. "As Passover Begins, Iran Fails to Pass Over the Holocaust: Stealth Jihad Thwarted—for the Moment—at UN Meeting." *www.jihadwatch.org* (posted April 10, 2009, accessed December 30, 2009).

——————. "Darfur Debacle at the UN Human Rights Council in Geneva." *www.jihadwatch.org* (posted December 16, 2007, accessed December 30, 2009).

Lynch, Colum. "Former UN Oil-for-Food Chief Indicted." *The Washington Post*, January 17, 2007.

——————. "Russia Won't Block Removal of Former Taliban Members from UN Terrorism List." *The Washington Post*, January 27, 2010.

Miskin, Maayana. "Almagor: UN Supports Terrorism." *Israel National News*, May 18, 2009.

Molinski, Dan. "Venezuela Has Leftist-Led Plans to Help Rebuild Haiti." *www.foxbusiness.com* (posted January 24, 2010, accessed January 25, 2010).

"Muslim Countries Win Concession Regarding Religious Debates." *Daily Times* (Pakistan), June 19, 2008. Associated Press dispatch.

Naiman, Robert. "UN: Time for Direct Talks with Afghan Taliban Leaders." *The Huffington Post*, January 27, 2010.

Paul, Ron. "Why Do We Fund UNESCO?" *www.proconservative.net* (posted July 23, 2005, accessed January 8, 2010).

"Peacekeepers 'Abusing Children.'" *news.bbc.co.uk* (posted May 27, 2008, accessed January 11, 2010).

Pearl, Judea. "Islam Struggles to Stake Out Its Position." *International Herald Tribune*, July 8, 2005, p. 8.

Quist, Allen. "Why International Baccalaureate (IB) Is Un-American." Education for a Free Nation website. *www.edwatch.org* (posted April 7, 2006, accessed January 20, 2010).

Rockas, Peter. "If the UN and Americans Do Not Fulfill the Wish of Our Religious Scholars Then Fatwas Will Follow." *www.jihadwatch.org* (Reuters dispatch, posted February 14, 2004, accessed February 1, 2010).

Rosenthal, Elisabeth. "UN Climate Panel and Chief Face Credibility Siege." *New York Times*, February 8, 2010.

Russell, George. "U.S. Ignored UN Aid Agency's Fraud and Mismanagement." *www.foxnews.com* (posted and accessed January 11, 2010).

Saunders, Lucy-Claire. "A Dangerous Proposition: *Negotiating with the Taliban*." *english.news.cn* (posted and accessed January 31, 2010).

Schlein, Lisa. "Secret Detention Violates International Humanitarian Law." Voice of America website. *www1.voanews.com* (posted and accessed January 27, 2010).

"The Sex Industry Is Growing in East Timor, as Traffickers Lure Women In." *www.theaustralian.com.au* (posted February 7, 2009, accessed January 12, 2010).

Shear, Michael D., and Dan Balz. "Obama Appeals for Global Cooperation." *www.washingtonpost.com* (posted September 24, 2009, accessed January 6, 2010).

Silverman, Anav. "The UN's New 'Factfinding' Mission." *Frontpagemagazine.com* (posted June 29, 2009, accessed December 21, 2009).

Spencer, Robert. "Free Speech Dies at the UN." International Analyst Network. *analyst-network.com* (posted June 26, 2008, accessed December 21, 2009).

Stein, Sam. "Axelrod: Obama Has Made Anti-Americanism Uncool." *www.huffingtonpost.com* (posted July 25, 2009, accessed January 4, 2010).

"UN Cuts Back on Investigating Its Own Fraud." *www.foxnews.com* (posted and accessed January 12, 2010).

"UN Haiti Troops Accused of Rape." *www.bbs.co.uk* (posted November 30, 2006, accessed January 11, 2010).

Urbina, Ian. "Ex-UN Weapons Inspector Is Charged in Child-Sex Sting." *The New York Times*, January 14, 2010.

Usborne, David. "How the UN Meeting Turned into a Festival of Anti-Americanism—and Boosted Dubya's Election Hopes." *The Independent*, September 23, 2006.

"Venezuela Leader Accuses DEA of Espionage." *www.foxnews.com* (posted August 7, 2005, accessed January 4, 2010).

"White House Slaps UN Secretary-General on 'Deadbeat' Comments." *blogs.abcnews.com* (posted March 12, 2009, accessed December 22, 2009).

Index

About the Author

Michael Benson is the author of the Citadel Books *Who's Who in the JFK Assassination: An A to Z Encyclopedia* and *Inside Secret Societies: What They Don't Want You to Know*. He is the former editor of the *Military Technical Journal*, *Warzone*, and *Untold Stories of Vietnam* magazines, and author of *Complete Idiot's Guides* to Submarines, Aircraft Carriers, NASA, the CIA, and National Security. Originally from Rochester, NY, he is a graduate of Hofstra University. He is married and lives in New York City.